BASS FISHING

A GUIDE TO MASTERING FRESHWATER BASS FISHING TECHNIQUES

CHRIS LUTZ

ISBN: 1532739508
ISBN-13: 978-1532739507

DEDICATION

I dedicate this book to my Dad.

CONTENTS

ACKNOWLEDGMENTS

I'd like to acknowledge all the anglers who came before me and contributed to the knowledge I've gained through their experience.

i

FRESHWATER BASS FISHING

Learn the basics. Play the angler's game of condition, circumstance, knowledge, opportunity, and skill.

Shape your own personal approach to catching fish. Often what I read in magazines or online, usually taken as fishing gospel, turns out not to be true for me in many cases. It can be due to a variety of factors like location in the country, daily conditions, and other local factors. But, in any case, it serves as a jumping off point for what has worked for others and then I refine for myself. If you keep that in mind, even with what I'm saying here, THEN you should catch more fish, bigger fish, and more often, regardless of conditions. You'll learn to navigate the interplay of other random factors that change daily. Synergize and strategize. Plan to succeed and you will.

This guide, will help, give you background information, handy tips, and pointers to ponder and try to master and enjoy!

What Are We Fishing For Again? The Target: Bass Defined

Whatever the reason you had for picking up these pages, to learn more about fishing, you are sure to find a quenching reprieve. There is something for everyone in this book!

If your main interest, is improving your ability to catch bass, increasing, (and maybe) even stacking the odds in your favor of succeeding, time and again, nearly every time, in any future expeditions you plan to undertake, then this book has something of value to offer you.

When you are on the hunt for bass, knowing the basics is the lifeblood of your strategy, bringing your chances of success closer with every cast!

Also, discover and develop your own sportsman-like angling style and character while gradually building your appreciation and understanding of the great outdoors as part of your fishing experience.

Fishing for and catching bass, in various waters across the globe, has a proud history and tradition. Most of us are too glad to be dabbling in any form of it, whether from boat, shore, rocks, rivers, streams, lakes, or oceans. We like to tell our tales and contemplate how to change, modify, adapt, and/or create new techniques, to hook smallmouth, largemouth, spotted, and striped bass. To each his own. You pick your favorite.

We present a practical approach to the intricacies and complexities involved in this popular sport. Our focus and goals are simple. The basis and premise even simpler: Learn the basics, get them right, consistently, with skill, and mastery. And that will eventually lead you to catching many fish over an angling lifetime.

I prefer to get right to the topic and elements of our discussion: How to find and catch bass. Most published works and accomplished authors (many anglers themselves), depict bass fishing as the ultimate angling experience and the bass, predator and hunter, itself, as tough, unpredictable, with a strong survival instinct, great awareness, and keen senses that make them the effective hunters they are.

These fish benefit from nature's gifts of powerful sight, hearing, fast speed, maneuverability, and even water pressure sensitivity, that will have you excited with adrenaline when you catch them. All of this makes it possible for the bass to live up to its name and reputation, as one of the most popular of the game fish populations and many an angler's dream catch.

Their food of choice and natural diet includes many things from small fish, crustaceans, worms, and insects, to even frogs, mice, and snakes. They are very opportunistic. Some anglers have also had great success with live-bait. Live lining a sun fish is a great way to potentially score a huge bass in a lake or pond.

Then there are the black bass, collectively referred to and including our prized target, called by some to be the most sporting species in North America, the *Centrarchidae* family. (Largemouth and smallmouth bass, redeye, spotted, Suwannee, Guadalupe).

Artificial baits have proven useful to most anglers. Live baits may be best, but these fish can be tempted, teased and lured to strike with artificial ones such as spinners, spoons, crank-baits, top water baits, and soft plastics. More on this a little later. Knowing which to choose (and why), which to switch to in certain conditions, and how to optimize this art of allure, is a key basic element for every aspiring angler.

These fish are all active predators, warming to natural baits and artificial lures. Most anglers would suggest spinning or casting equipment for freshwater fishing for bass (larger species) and spinning or fly fishing for the smaller species. Although fly fishing for big largemouth or smallmouth bass with 5-8 weight fly rods is becoming more and more popular too.

Knowing how to tell a smallmouth from a largemouth bass, striped from spotted and so on is a very basic skill most anglers master quickly. Looking specifically at size and physical features are good places to start. Train your eye to spot the differences, so to speak. These fish will overlap in habitat, but you may be more likely to catch one kind over another in certain locations. You'll never catch a largemouth or smallmouth out in a saltwater bodies of water, but may be in brackish areas. But, you will catch striped bass or stripers, as they are called. They are easily identifiable by their name sake rows of lateral stripes down their bodies.

Generally, the easiest way to tell them apart is a largemouth is greenish in color and a smallmouth is brownish in color. That's not always readily apparent on every fish especially in pictures. And telling a smallmouth apart from a red eye or a red eye apart from a warm mouth or a largemouth apart from a spotted bass is more difficult.

They differ in size, markings, mouth shape, and dorsal fins. Their upper jaws are different in length and their dorsal fins are not the same. The largemouth has a spiny dorsal fin, highest in the middle portion, with almost a distinct break, right before the second set of dorsal fins start. For the smallmouth bass, these fins are flatter, first and second are connected, with distinct scales at the base of the second set of dorsal fins.

Smallmouth bass can overlap territory with largemouth bass, but it's generally thought of as a riverine species. Smallmouth do inhabit large bodies of water like Lake Erie though as well.

Smallmouth bass typically inhabit the upper portions of rivers that are rockier and have swifter moving current. Largemouth are much more at home in ponds, lakes, and lower portions, or even tidal, rivers. You'll find both in many areas, but usually one species is dominating the population in one particular area.

Aside from knowing and telling your fish species apart by sights and or physical characteristics, there is some general advice we can propose right up front. Experiencing, treading lightly, and honoring nature, the great outdoors, abiding by catch and release laws, and environmental protection for the generations of anglers to come, are all vastly important in your angling endeavors.

Second, maintain an overall alertness. What some call "reading the water" (understanding the body of water, structure, cover, habitat of the fish, contours, depth, temperature, stratified levels, seeing current). Be generally, as well as specifically observant, arming yourself with knowledge, skill, and understanding of the fish. The species, the environment, and all other relevant factors to your fishing are paramount for a successful process and outcome.

Third, (and almost most importantly), remain adaptable. Change is a big part of this enjoyable outdoor activity. It is definitely not for the faint of heart or the impatient among us. But, if it wasn't challenging, it wouldn't be fun. I know certain guys that will tie on some specific baits and won't change them no matter what the fish and conditions are telling them. That may be fine, and I do it too, if I'm trying to build my confidence and skill with certain baits.

I spoke with another angler recently who posted five pictures of nice sized walleye online. He was in a bass tournament and was "disappointed" in the fact that he wasn't catching what he was after. He asked, what would you do? I said I'd say to hell with the tournament and have a great day walleye fishing. But, that's me. I'm not a tournament guy. In his particular situation it was a problem. But, if you're out there for recreation, the fish may be telling you something. Your bass fishing may have just turned into a walleye fishing trip despite fishing for bass. Outside of a tournament, I doubt many anglers could still come back to the ramp without a smile on their face after that.

Some days are just like that. Your target species just isn't in the mood or can't be found for one reason or another. In most instances, you want to listen to what you're subtly being told, don't try to dictate the situation yourself.

THE BASICS OF BASS FISHING

Most, if not all of the so-called insider secrets, tips, and stories to tell of big hauls of bass, all revolve, around a very simple basic rule, understanding the fish. Their life-cycles, feeding preferences, habits, patterns, menu of choice, their nature, their relationship with the broader eco-system, and position on the food-chain. Also heeding your surroundings, your equipment, having the know-how and basics under your belt and finally optimizing every opportunity.

In effect, you are going about creating the most favorable angling process and outcome you can muster.

Bass fishing is a passion, a science, and an art form in itself. It appeals to young and old, attracts anglers from all walks of life and both sides of the professional and amateur spectrum.

One key to bass fishing is what we can easily refer to as, predictable behavior. Habits, patterns, life cycles, the natural rhythm that is life, and nature also applies to fish. This means that bass exist within this natural reality that you and I do too. If you can capitalize on understanding it better, you will increase your chances of successful bites.

Seeking protective cover, foraging amongst rocks, stumps, weeds, at times on the prowl hunting for prey, other times just lunching around casually, all seem to be part of bass feeding rituals and repertoire. Taking advantage and considering this when starting out will benefit you greatly.

Another is "competitive advantage", the bass has an air sac swim bladder that is inflatable, which enables it to swim and thrive at different levels. A powerful tail helps with speed, agility, and maneuverability. It can reach great depths.

Other factors like water clarity, time of day, subdued sunlight, water displacement and vibration sensing, noise sensitivity, all add to this fish' cunning and ensuring that you scrutinize these clues, will increase your odds of hooking your next big one.

Unlocking the bass' senses and preferred colors and shades in the moment, can always help anglers increase their effectiveness. The choice and type of lure, colors, movement, and bait can all contribute meaningfully to your attempts.

Where are the fish? Everyone will have an answer, or at least their opinion, on what/where/when, even the science. Nevertheless, sometimes it is as simple as understanding the habitat and those that live and thrive in it, to better interact with and enjoy fishing in it. A type of exploring the depths, so to speak. For example: the temperature of the water and available oxygen, dictate moving patterns and disbursement of fish species.

Feeding habits and preferences are distinct, falling more on the "looking alive" or live bait. Some quote smallmouth bass, as showing preference for crawfish and using that as a sign of where these fish will be found on the hunt for their favorite snack. Looking at stomach contents of fish you have caught and kept (not part of the catch and release protocol/requirements), hold hidden clues about food of preference bait fish, crawfish, and others.

Having self-confidence and the right attitude when fishing for bass is crucial. In this battle to outwit your opponent, you will need every tool and trick at your disposal to make a successful catch. Never get discouraged, feel beaten, or worse quit for the yield has been slim to none at all. Those days happen to every angler more often than not. Nature beats to its own drum. You have to discover and enjoy the rhythm you are so intricately part of at any given moment.

Practice makes perfect. There is no silver bullet, quick-fish method that can guarantee you bites and more bass all the time, anytime. It does take hard work, commitment, and persistence from the angler. There is more than routine at work here. Don't make the mistake of hopping from place to place as some anglers do as though the next place is going to magically be where all the fish start biting your lures. Take the time to learn individual spots. Some days will be predictably better than others. No matter what the conditions and outcome, on the day, put it all down to experience and lessons learned. Log and learn. Share and grow, in your own understanding, confidence, and toolbox, as an avid fisherman.

Another key is actually no trick at all. We call it an acquired skill. It takes more of that hard work we mentioned before. Exact, fixed casting, requires target-precision practice. Improving your ability to place the lure exactly where you would want it to be. Let us call it hitting the mark. This is another crucial tactic and technique you can practice in the park or some other open space. Try using plugs and get better every time at consistently hitting your target.

Here's an example. I had caught several nice largemouths off a bank in the river the day before I went out there with my Dad. I assumed they might be there again. They were. I wanted to give my Dad the first cast. I told him exactly where to place it. He had a slightly lighter lure on than I did and didn't get as much distance. I told him again to get it almost exactly one foot from the shore then pull it slowly off the bank.

Another short cast and nothing. I casted up there and immediately pulled three more nice largemouth off the bank. He couldn't believe it. So I stopped casting and said again to get it closer to the bank, almost exactly a foot away, and this time he nailed it and pulled off a nice largemouth for himself. Even small details like casting 12 inches outside your target can make a big difference in your success.

If you're not a detail oriented person, you likely won't see or realize that. But, there is a LOT of detail that goes into fishing techniques. Much of it takes years to practice and learn. You think that extra foot on the cast doesn't matter? It does. You think the fish will just come to your bait? They won't. You think that extra little bit of tag end hanging off the clinch knot on your hook doesn't matter? It does. Not all the time, but many times, getting everything right is what is needed in order to get a fish to bite. We'll get to more specific technique details a little later.

Becoming and being a proactive participant in the context and environment, knowing when to move on, change something, or quit for the time being, postponing the hunt, or resting when required, planning your strategy for the next trip out, is what it is all about as well.

Habitual creatures of comfort, bass as a species, are not so much different than modern man. Bearing this in mind will help you as an angler. We like what we like, when and how we like it. And normally want it on time. We want to feel safe, enjoy life, and we crave comfort. Food, shelter, and well-being! Does this sound a lot different from our own needs and requirements? Not really. Well, that is one way of leveling the playing field. Understanding the basic necessities and niceties for these watery creatures, holds clues for every angler.

Stimulus, pattern, routine, are habit are predictors and hints, the ace up your sleeve when nothing else works. Learn and develop skills, to read the situation. Observe and make a judgment. Know instinctively what will come next and why. Figure out the pattern. Stick with it and exploit it to your advantage and angling success. Meet the fish where they are, in what they do, cater to their needs, and you will be surprised at what meets you get.

Familiarity with the Bass' favorite places to hang around is critical to success. Bottoms, stumps, trees, logs, weeds, plants, contours, structures, travel-routes, creeks, shallows, deeper passages, coves, channels, bluffs, banks and shorelines all can be habitually frequented spots. This offers you a predictable behavior of the bass. Most of the experts came about their knowledge through reading, studying habits of their catch, in very similar fashion of what you are doing now.

Every time you get to know your fish quarry a little better, until you know almost instinctively where they will be and where their favorite spots are. Knowing and going where the fish are becomes demystified, but even more exciting. Now it is more than a hunch or random chance. It is a planned encounter where the watery predator, hunter becomes the hunted. You will start to anticipate a strike more now that more of your actions are specifically directed rather than casting aimlessly which you may have done before.

TACKLE AND LURES

Rod Selection

There isn't a more important tool for accomplishing your goal of catching more fish (other than a boat) than the fishing rod, itself.

To me, a good all-purpose design for freshwater bass fishing might look something like this:

- A reasonable length handle for casting leverage, but not so long as to interfere with retrieval techniques
- Split foam handle
- Light weight-Won't weigh down your boat if you carry many rods
- Balanced
- Medium action-For sensitivity and pulling largemouth bass out of cover or strong fighting small mouths out of river grass or ledge rock
- 7'-For casting small lures a long distance
- 1/8 – 3/4 oz. bait weight range
- 8 – 15# line rating. Up to 30# braid can be used
- Spinning and/or bait casting option

The rod described above is our choice for something like a medium power worm rod. I'll have other technique specific rods including a seven foot, medium-light, fast action crawfish rod or small jig rod.   And a seven foot, medium-light, moderate action, swimbait/crankbait rod to name a few.

The more moderate action of a swimbait/crankbait rod will help you in keeping the fish on during the fight.   Fish can often use leverage to unhook themselves.   The more forgiving nature of a moderate action shaft keeps the treble hooks embedded in the fish's mouth instead of having something more rigid to gain leverage on like a faster action rod and non-stretchable braided line.

Sometimes, you may encounter a paradox or compromise of sorts.   An angler's paradox, perhaps.   A suspending jerk bait has treble hooks.   Do you go with the moderate action rod to keep the fish on during the fight? Or do you go with the faster action to be able to impart the darting, slashing, walking presentation on the lures to get the fish to bite in the first place.   You can see how you can't do both at the same time.

In this case, we usually opt for the fast action rod, with non-stretch braided line to be able to impart the needed action on the lure. It's probably more important that your presentation is correct. Without that, there won't be any fish to land in the first place. So you attempt to land the fish even though he may have slightly more advantage now with a stiffer rod and small treble hooks.

Having the right equipment, knowing how to best use it, when and how, (also how not to use it and what it is not suitable for), can all help you in your bass fishing adventure.

The basics regarding rods, reels, line, hooks, weights, bobbers, sinkers, lures, and other equipment (hats, PFD's, nets, scents, scissors etc.), gives you an appreciation for having the right tools for the task(s) at hand.

As a highly participatory and engaging sport, fishing is simply almost unparalleled in the vast amount of styles and tools to use. From quiet streams, tranquil lakes to open water and rushing rivers, there is something for everyone.

If you are looking for quick tips on the right equipment, most suited to your purpose and the techniques to master to catch bass in any conditions, might this next section enlighten and inspire you, as you delve right into the utilities of the fishing trade. Some tools of the bass fishing trade, we will be focusing on.

Limited space does not permit large comparative explanations or ramblings on the merit of some tools above certain others. These debates are well known and well published in existing literature. We take a more practical approach and look at what you will actually need to hook your next fish, besides random chance and luck. We like to point out that picking the right equipment means a lot of different things to different people. Each angler has his/her own interpretation of what that means, varying skill level, physical characteristics, budgets, and strengths/weaknesses. So we will not profess knowing what is right for you. What we do offer are mere suggestions on which tools will stack the odds in your favor and help you enjoy preparing, rigging, baiting, hooking, retrieving, and landing your next big one. Ensuring that it does not join the droves of "the one that got away"!

As you explore your surroundings and the wonder of fish species and their life cycles, patterns, and behavior, experimenting hands-on with your equipment, and what is available to anglers today, is part of the exciting world of fishing. From fish-finders, temperature gauges, sensors, and more advanced technologies, to the art of preparing your lines and hooks, choosing the lures most suited to your circumstance and purpose and more, adds to the excitement and enjoyment of the activity. Preparing yourself with knowledge on these, will boost your confidence and practicing often, will pay off in the long run as your expertise, exposure and angling mastery grows.

When it comes to equipment, the opinions are many. Your conditions, circumstances, purpose, and goal will all figure into the final choice (oh, yes and do not forget the ever-present budget and affordability).

Spinning or bait casting with artificial lures, fly-fishing, trolling with live-baits, are all options available to you, with specialist tools on hand to assist you in making the most of it. Typically a 6.5 to 7 feet rod (spinning or bait casting), with a matching reel with six to ten pound line, fast taper, single action reel would serve you well. Weedless hooks or rigs are a lifesaver in very dense cover or weeds.

Angling techniques and tackle keep refining, developing, and almost takes on a life of their own for every angler. There is not really a one-size-fits-all approach. This personalized relationship with your equipment, might mean a basic rod to start with and then adding a couple specialized ones for your different excursions and expeditions. Modern tackle and methods, traditional or innovative, technology-driven and enabled, whatever your fancy or preference, there is something for every taste and budget.

It is an ancient sport, pursued by many, with echoes of early hunters and anglers living off the land. Getting in touch with that timeline through hands-on activity, like bass fishing is very rewarding. Most beginners might be overwhelmed by the selection of equipment available on the market today. Knowing what to pick and buy, how and when to apply, how to use it correctly, how to maximize your chances of success is key.

Good quality tackle is important. It needs to be adequate for whatever nature throws your way. You will need to build your arsenal of knowledge and equipment over time, to respond best to some of the challenges at hand. Good baits and lures and how to use them effectively, in combination, maybe in quick succession, to ensure bites. As is the importance of preparing, presenting well, accurate casting, setting the hook, as well as retrieving and landing of the fish.

All we will say, is that having expensive or the right equipment, is not a guarantee that you will land any fish. In fishing, there are no real guarantees. This is an activity between you and nature. Exploring and getting you to the point where you know the feel, function, and integral strengths and weaknesses of your equipment, is the real way to wisdom. For most trial and error, practice and persistence are the roads to follow to becoming well-versed and experienced anglers.

Realizing the equipment's full potential will take time and practice. Bear in mind, that sophistication in equipment will develop in parallel to your own mastery and skill refinement.

Your intended style of fishing will dictate the most appropriate choice for tackle, boat, reel, rod, line, hooks, baits, lures, weights, sinkers, leaders, and more.

Whether you are a saltwater fanatic that enjoys shore or beach launch, big-game fishing, or a freshwater guy, there are rods, reels, line, hooks, leaders, baits, and landing tackle just right for you.

Basic angling techniques are relatively easy to master, yet conquering and refining all the subtleties and intricate moves and maneuvers, exploring the secrets discovered or yet to be discovered, will take a lifetime of pleasure and challenge.

Practice and enjoy bass fishing, according to your own niche and style, preference and location of choice, in a word, your "specialty." It is a very personalized and individualized pursuit and passion. Always remember, that there is a wide array of variety and enjoyment on offer, by different kinds of fishing, locations, baits and lures etc., to keep angling interesting and a growing sport – it is contagious and pervasive – once let in, it is hard to let go! You are hooked and being reeled in by this sport and hobby before you know it.

For most anglers, technique (and choice of equipment) is dictated by the species sought, established practice, conditions and more. Mostly artificial lures are suggested and accepted for freshwater predatory fishing. Some prefer live bait, others have success with hard baits like crankbaits or poppers.

Whether you are fishing from the banks, kayak, bass boat, or float tube, most would suggest you use a six to seven foot medium, spinning or bait-casting rod and reel combination, with somewhat strong line (8-10-pound). If you are fishing in weeds, heavy cover, thick, slop, grassy wetlands, swamps a heavier line (braid), will serve you better.

Apart from your own custom design, some of the most popular and in demand rods that have similar specifications are St. Croix fishing rods.

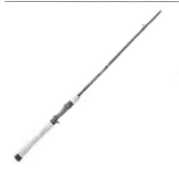

The St. Croix Legend Elite Casting Rod.

http://bit.ly/23EoWwX

The St. Croix Avid Series in casting or spinning.

http://bit.ly/1qoISVK

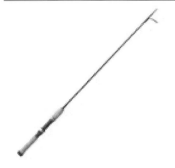

The St. Croix Premier Series in spinning or casting can be a very high quality rod that is matched with affordability.

http://bit.ly/1No8N5p

What may be the ultimate in affordability, durability, and performance, might be the Ugly Stick GX2 models in either spinning or casting versions. I really like that you can put the rod through hell and it's virtually indestructible. Even the guides have been replaced with no inserts so they don't pop out with such frequency. It's a good mix of fiberglass and graphite for lightness and sensitivity as well as durability. The seven foot, medium power, fast action should be applicable to many general freshwater fishing scenarios.

http://bit.ly/23uevzb

Reels

If given the opportunity to have a bad rod and a good reel or a good rod and a bad reel, I'd choose the good rod. The reel could be argued to be much less important. It could be a soda can on the other end of the line and all it has to do is wind it back in for you. Some anglers prefer certain brands or the manufacturing components of one reel over another. Some prefer how the drag operates. Or even the durability or corrosion resistance. Some like the lightness or smoothness of certain reels. I tend to prefer durability first. You can make your own decisions regarding which aspects of reels you like. But, many would agree that a good rod may take precedence over a high priced reel in most instances.

For normal bass fishing, spinning tackle, here too, we want to go as light as we can get away with. Even small, light-duty reels can land the occasional monster. As mine did when a big blue catfish hit my small spoon I was trolling. I landed him on a medium light rod with 8 pound fluoro leader and 10 pound braided line.

A reel that is a 5.2:1 retrieve ratio and can hold six to 12 pound line is probably about right for a general freshwater spinning outfit.

Generally, Shimano, Diawa, Quantum, and Abu Garcia all make good spinning reels.

A higher level, quality spinning reel I like is the Quantum Smoke.

http://bit.ly/1Mu0nP3

A mid-level reliable spinning reel is something like the Abu Garcia Orra 2S.

http://bit.ly/1S6xcOZ

The Bass Pro Extreme spinning reel has some interesting design features and qualities; a larger spool for less line twist and casting distance, light, and smooth. And at a very attractive price point.

http://bit.ly/2bBxSy1

And some of the most durable reels ever made that are definitely on the lower end of the affordability spectrum are Mitchell reels. Like the Mitchell 300 series. My father still has old Mitchell reels that are older than I am and dinosaurs by today's standards, but still work and are likely to outlive us all.

http://bit.ly/1qoL0Nt

For casting reels, I prefer to have a 6.2:1 retrieve ratio reel for general duty, but also a 7.2:1 higher geared "burner" reel for faster retrieves of swimbaits and crankbaits. The lower geared reel allows you to use it, in combination with heavier line and heavier powered rods, to winch fish out of slop, cover, structure you may be fishing. If you try to do that with a higher geared reel, it won't work as well. It's like trying to get your manual transmission car rolling in fourth gear rather than first.

The numbers indicate how many spool turns to how many cranks of the spinning reel handle. So 5 spool turns to every 1 crank of the handle is a faster retrieve than 4:1. This really has to do with speed versus power. The closer you are to 1:1, the more power it will have. The greater the difference between the two numbers, the more speed it will have.

A higher end bait caster reel that is light and low profile would be exemplified by the Shimano Curado low profile.

http://bit.ly/1N8odzP

Here too for a mid to higher end bait caster reel, I like the Quantum Smoke PT low profile.

http://bit.ly/1Q6N01G

An affordable lower end bait caster would be something like the Bass Pro Shops MegaCast Low-Profile Bait cast Reel.

http://bit.ly/1Q6N9Cn

Most of the difference between higher end or better made bait casting rods may turn out to be castability. Some people have tried lower end bait caster thinking they couldn't get the skill down and try a friend's higher end model and it turns out to be night and day in terms of their acquisition of performing the cast and feathering the reel spool so as not to backlash. Take a little more time assessing your options for bait casters than you might for spinning reels. If possible, try them out first.

Most spinning reels today are made left hand retrieve. You crank the handle with your left hand while holding the rod with your right. The majority also make it easy to switch the reel handle to the other side if the angler prefers. This is not so with casting reels. Most casting reels are made right hand retrieve. Most anglers are right handed so this creates a situation where they cast as they normally would with their right hand on the reel, but then must switch hands as the lure hits the water to begin retrieving. This is one of those things that has never really made sense to me. I prefer consistency here between the two styles. Although they are harder to find, there are left hand retrieve casting reels.

I prefer not to switch hands at one of the most important parts of the angling process where I could miss a fish. Biomechanically speaking, my right hand is my dominant hand and, therefore, the most skilled. I prefer to do the techniques of fishing with my dominant hand on the rod rather than my non-dominant hand which might end up with a less than ideal lure presentation on the other end of the line. That's just my preference. If you prefer the same, be sure to look for the left hand retrieve bait casting reels as they are harder to find and less standard.

Lines

Any beginner angler can get by with normal, monofilament fishing line, in the right poundage for the rod and reel they are using, and fish species, they are fishing for. Recently we've seen advancements in so-called super lines and hybrids such as a fluorocarbon coated monofilament.

It is worth noting that the line, and specifically any knots you tie are going to be the weakest link between you and possibly a big fish. So be sure to match all the parts of your gear together for the task at hand.

In general, there are three types of line. There could be more classifications, but we'll stick with three to make this section easy.

Monofilament. This is what your father used. It's the old standby. It is cheap and plentiful and comes in a variety of sizes, strengths, colors, and volumes. It can perform nearly any fishing task. This is all we had for some time. Its cons lie in the fact that it has memory, meaning, it will retain a shape it has been forced into for some time (coiled on a reel spool in the off season). It stretches. You may not want that when trying to jerk bait fish, for instance, or have a high degree of sensitivity. It floats. And its abrasion resistance isn't as good as fluorocarbon.

Sunline, has a good brand of monofilament that doesn't stretch as much, casts, and handles well. If you get it in clear or green, in the six to twelve pound range, this makes for a good monofilament fishing outfit.

http://bit.ly/1YtuarO

Fluorocarbon looks a lot like monofilament, but it has higher abrasion resistance. Some kinds are less visible in water. These two facts make it a good leader material choice. It is more expensive. It doesn't stretch. And it sinks. It might be a small detail, but using fluorocarbon with a floating top water bait, might not make the best combination as fluoro can sink. Fluoro also has less memory, but that also makes it want to come off of spinning reel spools easier.

Berkley's Vanish fluoro in the six to twelve pound range can be an excellent bass fishing application especially when you need to go light or when the fish are line shy. I keep a small spool in my PFD all the time for less visible leader material.

http://bit.ly/23EtMdn

Copolymer is a line that has a blend of these materials. Often it is monofilament with a fluorocarbon coating. It has better knotting capability, more abrasion resistance, and less stretch. Essentially, you can get some of the benefits of fluorocarbon, but for a few less bucks.

Something like P-Line Copolymer Floroclear represents this class of line well. A spool of this in the six to twelve pound test range in clear is good for most spinning freshwater applications.

http://bit.ly/2bRTojF

Braided lines. There are all kinds of braided lines on the market now. These are the most expensive, but the most durable and long lasting. They allow for a much smaller diameter line for the given strength. It allows for the most sensitivity. The poundage rating is usually much higher than posted on the box. It is more visible in the water and does float. It is hard to cut with nail clippers. You may need a special line cutter like what is in the joint of some pliers to cut braid effectively. It is subject to catching wind. Thicker lines can get water logged and tend to loop up when retrieved on spinning reels. It knots very easily and very tightly. It has a much thinner diameter as the same strengths of mono or fluoro. It casts very far. It is hard to break off. Sometimes you want to break off. If you get a hard snag while boating in moving water, you don't want the line to be so strong you can't quickly get out of that situation. Worse, you don't want to become entangled in it, yourself, at all, or in the water. It is very thin in diameter and can cut into your skin under pressure.

I used two kinds of braid. The most well-known and reliable is probably PowerPro. I use it in the 10-15 pound test range for castability and either the hi-vis yellow or moss green depending on what I am doing.

http://bit.ly/1Sadcgu

The other kind I like is Spiderwire EZ Braid. This has a little more of a slick outer appearance and I think casts slightly better, but seems it may twist more on spinning reels.

http://bit.ly/1T3PL8M

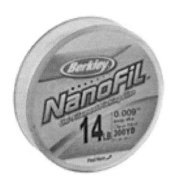

Other lines like Berkley's Nanofil or Sufix could fall into the super line category and may have some characteristics of the others mixed in. Berkley's nanofil is neither braid nor mono or fluoro. It's a compound they call uni-filament made from Dyneema.

http://bit.ly/1TR9fzF

Sufix 832 Advanced is braid, but a mix of fiber types and rounder weaving pattern.

http://bit.ly/1VUUJag

Most of the fishing I do involves some aspect of all of these line types. A normal freshwater bass fishing set up would involve the rod and reel selection above coupled with a monofilament backing on the reel to either an Albright or double Uni knot to braided line as the main line. It's important to have mono backing so as not to use up so much braid, but also to make sure it doesn't slip on your reel spool under tension. From the main braided line down to a short three to six foot length of about eight pound test fluorocarbon or copolymer, ultimately to the hook or lure.

Each line can have its own place according to what you're doing and what you'll be fishing for. Casting braided line on bait caster reels is somewhat tougher unless you go up into the higher poundages and thicker diameters.

Weights and Sinkers

These are another element you must consider, especially in dark, cloudy waters and or when fishing deep water specifically. There are also specialty sinkers, with rattles, these days to entice the fish even more. Fish are very sensitive to sounds, noise and vibrations in the water so anything you can do to create that allure is great to bear in mind or to avoid if you want a silent presentation.

Sinkers traditionally come in lead, but also come in newer materials like tungsten. Weights and sinkers have many varying shapes and sizes to match your fishing techniques.

For most bass fishing applications, I love using the Water Gremlin Bull Shot Split Bullet Weights. These are very similar to other bullet weights, but they don't slip and have a split so you don't have to cut the line and retie to add or remove one or change sizes.

http://bit.ly/1XvhmAR

Weights and sinkers also come in other shapes such as:

- Round split shot
- Bell sinkers
- Egg shaped sinkers
- Bank sinkers
- Pyramid shaped sinkers
- Coin shaped sinkers
- And specific drop shot weights

More often than not, we tend to stick with bullet, egg, and split shot in freshwater fishing. Sinkers can be tied on mid line as you would with a Carolina rig, clamped on with a split weight, pegged in place with a tooth pick for a slip sinker, and allowing the sinker to freely slip up and down the line through its middle hole.

Here again, you want to use the right amount of weight for the application you'll be employing, but no more. Wind, current, and depth will all play a role. I find in most river or lake environments, I can get away with anything from weightless baits to 1/16th oz to about ¼ oz weights. 1/8th is my go to weight selection to fish the bottom of a shallow river, lake, or pond.

Snaps, Snap-swivels, Swivels

These items are what is known as terminal tackle. In addition to being mindful of things like how line shy your fishing target may be, the same holds true for things like snaps. A snap may make it very easy to change baits, and that can be a good thing so you don't have to constantly retie or keep cutting off more of your leader. However, it can also add an element of artificiality to your lure that is already artificial. Fish can be snap shy too. It could mean the difference between nothing and a few more caught fish. If I am some place and only have one rod or so, I may use snaps to help me change baits and pattern the fish. I usually try to use them with moving baits too. Something I'm not going to go low and slow with and sit in front of the fish for a long time to allow them to get a good look at it. Snaps can fail too.

I notice with some of the gold colored snaps on the market, the metal fails rather quickly or falls apart completely. You don't want to lose a good fish just because of some poor metal manufacturing. Additionally, the more metal tackle you have at the end of your line, the more things can get hung up on it. Some snaps have a small wire tag end that protrudes out of the wire gate. Although this adds strength to the snap closure, it is also a great place to hang up grass, weeds, and algae. Most fish will not bite your lure if you're trailing a big green string of algae behind it. In weedy or grassy areas, you may consider going without this kind of snap.

Snap-swivels are exactly what they say. They can allow the quick change of baits, but also include a barrel swivel. This can be useful in not adding twist to your line. The swivel allows the bait to turn freely 360 degrees. If that swivel were not in place, and you had a bait that tended to turn in circles, eventually, you'll probably end up with a good amount of line twist you'll need to remove. Retrieving or trolling spoons that spin will add twist to your line if you don't have a snap swivel or swivel only in place. Some spoons come with their own, but more than likely, you'll need to add one to your line in order to fish the spoon.

Swivels or barrel swivels do not include the snap feature. These are usually placed further up the line and may attach the main line to the swivel and the leader line to the other end of the swivel. The same function applies by allowing it to freely rotate and avoid line twist, but could also be used concurrently for other things like a bobber stop, a place to attach a weight, something for a plastic bead to clack against, or place to add a secondary line. A three way swivel is useful if you have secondary lines tied to the main line.

A simple interlocking snap with wire gate.

http://bit.ly/1S6AVvI

An interlocking snap combined with a barrel swivel.

http://bit.ly/1N8qon7

The barrel swivel only option.

http://bit.ly/1RTY6NI

There's always a time and a place for using terminal tackle or not. More times than not, I'm trying to go without it. I usually have a freshwater bass fishing set up with one of the rods and reels selected from above, with 10 or 12 pound mono backing, tied in a double uni knot to 15 pound braid for the main line, tied in a double uni knot to an eight pound fluorocarbon leader, tied directly to the hook or lure usually with an improved clinch knot.

Go Here to View a Video on How to Remove Line Twist While Fishing

https://youtu.be/wRpHSaHWUPw

Hooks

There are all kinds of hooks and sizes and little standardization in sizes. The numbers remain the same, but the actual sizes from one manufacturer may not match the actual size of another.

Additionally, whole numbered sized hooks get smaller the greater the number. A #32 hook is the smallest. A 20/0 hook is the biggest. A #4 hook is bigger than a #32. But, a 4/0 hook is smaller than a 20/0. They run on either side of zero. There is no zero sized hook.

There are different thicknesses or gauges of the wire that make up the hook. Usually referred to as light wire or heavy wire.

The hook designs are made with the type of fishing and the target species in mind. There are live bait hooks, J-hooks, barbed hooks, unbarbed hooks, octopus, wide gap, extra wide gap, skip gap, circle, double, and treble. And more.

If you are using treble hooks, try removing some of the hooks so the damage to the fish is less. You can cut off one or two of the hooks or some anglers take the treble off and replace it with a single hook. Also try using circle hooks if you are using live bait. Just remember to not "set the hook" as much as you would with other hooks. When you get a bite just lift the rod tip to tighten the line up and start reeling, the hook will set itself in the corner of the fish's mouth, usually.

Hook sizes typically recommended around a #4 live-bait hook, sharpened and turned up slightly (say around 10%), this is done to ensure that the fish stayed hooked and gives you a fighting chance to reel it in and land it successfully. A weedless, #5 hook can also serve you well in these conditions. Largemouth bass can be caught at any depth, using a variety of baits, throughout most the year. Sharp hooks are key though. Even if the rest of your tackle is sub-par, make sure your hooks are quality and sharp!

One of the things many fishermen neglect is hook care. Have you ever lost a big fish that was on and wondered why? Maybe, your hook wasn't sharp.

If you fish brush piles, gravel beds, rock piles, log jams, bridge pilings, timber and boat docks you need to check your hooks for sharpness. A sharpening tool should be a regular part of your tackle box or can easily be put in a pocket of your PFD. I have mine there and pull it out regularly. If you're on your way to fish and don't have a sharpener go to a drug store and get a diamond-dust nail file at a drug store. It's important to check your hooks sharpness every time you get snagged.

Here is the way I test my hooks for sharpness:

Grab the shank of the hook in one hand and gently put the point on your thumbnail, don't apply any force or pressure whatsoever. Now, try and move the hook across your thumbnail, if the point digs in then the hook is sharp.

I also use this method for my knives to test their sharpness. Just drag your thumbnail across the blade at 90 degrees or a little less and it should shave off some of your nail if sharp. If it glides over your nail, you have a rounded or dulled edge.

Sharp hooks can make your fishing trip a success or failure. The big one doesn't have to get away when you have a sharp hook.

The VMC WM Worm hook is an excellent option for Texas rigging soft plastics on light tackle.

http://bit.ly/1qRRC7c

VMC hooks have a couple of unique features. The eyelet of the hook is covered with a resin to prevent line from slipping through or off. This is a small thing, but if I could have back every moment my knot got hung up on the opening of the hook eye, I'd have been a lot more efficient fisherman. Just a small thing makes a significant difference over time.

The other feature I like is the slightly offset hook point which can translate into better hook ups rather than the point and the shank being in the same plane. You see this a lot with circle hooks in saltwater tackle, but VMC has brought it to bass fishing.

Hot Weather Gear

When you're out exposed to the elements during a long day of fishing, it's critical that you protect yourself from those elements so that you can stay comfortable and enjoy what you're doing. And most of all so that you don't adversely affect your health.

During the hotter months, you'll have 2 concerns, heat and the sun, itself. The best gear for battling both elements while remaining functional for fishing is Columbia's P.F.G. (Performance Fishing Gear) line. Specifically, their items with Omni-shade for light weight sun protection. And Omni-freeze for sweat activated cooling.

Columbia's Omni-shade has long sleeve, high SPF sun protection while being light weight and fishing functional.

http://bit.ly/2bxHQ6n

Columbia's Backcast Convertible pants with Omni-shade offers the SPF sun protection while being light weight and quick drying. And can be converted into regular shorts.

http://bit.ly/2bjDQT3

Cold Weather Gear

Cold weather, and especially cold water can kill and quickly. Cold can be equally as deadly as heat, but it can occur much faster. It's critical that you equip yourself properly if there's the possibility of being submerged in a cold water fishing scenario. This would particularly be true for something like kayak fishing. You'll generally want at least three layers. You want to start with a wicking, light weight base layer. Next, you want an insulating layer. Finally, a protective outer layer that may be a full dry suit.

Stohlquist makes a very affordable unisex dry suit now that can accommodate winter anglers on a budget.

http://bit.ly/2bOOdjs

If there's little chance of immersion, if you'll be standing on a boat all day, you can use the same wicking and insulating under layers and go with outer protection with something like Bass Pro Shops' Gore Tex Rain Suit.

You can get the parka and the bibs together for full coverage.

http://bit.ly/2bCP0ry

Electronics

You'll likely need some kind of electronics like a fish finder, possibly a radio, and GPS. Scotty also makes a mount for fish finders which can easily be attached to any Scotty base whereever is most convenient on your deck.

I like the ease and versatility of the new Raymarine Dragonfly-4dv fish finder. It really takes all the guess work out of reading sonar.

http://bit.ly/2bQwEAn

You may be in an area that requires you to have a portable marine VHF radio. The portable ICOM M36 marine radio is a very popular and good option.

http://amzn.to/2bPrx2s

For smaller water, but a place where you still may want to talk freely with your fishing buddies in other boats, a simple two way walkie talkie set works great. This set from Uniden is submersible for up to 1 meter for 30 minutes. They also float should they go overboard. But, do come with carabiners for lanyards and head sets for hands free use.

http://amzn.to/1SGFxrM

If you'll need GPS on a regular basis, your best bet may be to get a combination unit that has sonar and GPS like the Humminbird Helix 5. In this day and age, you would be hard pressed to find a fishing boat without some sort of fish finding device. GPS devices have become the latest in technology and water safety when it comes to fishing. They are used as a means of navigation and a way to mark your spot so that you can find it again in the future.

A GPS is a Global Positioning System that is made primarily for navigational purposes. They work off a network of satellites that are placed into orbit by the United States Government. The best part about a GPS system is that because they operate off satellite, they can be used in any weather conditions at any hour of the day.

The satellites will circle the earth twice during the day and transmit signal information to Earth. The signals can then be used to calculate the user's exact location by implementing triangulation and pinpointing near exact spots. Triangulation means that the GPS receiver must be locked into three spots before a calculation of longitude and latitude can be displayed. After the satellites have mapped the location, the GPS can narrow in on other satellites for useful information such as speed, track, trip distance, destination distance and sunrise or sunset times.

The accuracy of the GPS system is pretty acute because of the multi-channel designs that are available. A GPS will lock onto a satellite and maintain that lock through one of their channels. A GPS fish finder is accurate up to fifteen meters while the newer models increase in accuracy up to three meters.

There are many benefits to investing in a GPS and people are using GPS more regularly and relying on them more than the more traditional ways of navigation on the water. If you have plot points that you have saved on a GPS, you may be able to save time and frustration on the open water by going directly to the location that had the fish the last time you went out. Another advantage to the GPS is that it can detect hot fishing spots that may not be detected by older maps or charts. In addition, if you find a perfect fishing spot, you can share it with a friend when you go fishing with them or tell them over the radio. But, be careful not to give your best spots away to everyone.

GPS systems are also a great safety tool when you are out on the water. People will easily be turned around or lost and a GPS is an easy tool to use to find your way back home. You can also use a GPS system if there is unexpected bad weather such as fog or heavy rain. Some GPS systems are also equipped with mapping software that makes it easier to find a dock or other refuge. The GPS is accurate enough that it is able to communicate exact positions to the Coast Guard or rescue crew if an emergency arises.

You can purchase a handheld GPS online or at your local marine or boating store. A small mount can be attached to your boat to hold the device and keep it in your line of sight while you navigate.

You should never rely on just one navigation tool when you are fishing. A GPS seems to cover all of the bases, but it is still a computerized tool. You should always be proactive about your safety and always have marine maps and charts onboard at all times if you'll be in such environments.

http://amzn.to/1W3F60b

Or a smaller handheld device like the highly popular Garmin GPSMAP 78sc Waterproof Marine GPS and Chart plotter.

http://amzn.to/2bjO4D7

A small GPS mount or cradle positioned close to or beside your fish finder will be a useful addition. These can be mounts secured to the deck with hardware or by suction cup. Just be sure the suction cup has a good lock and that your GPS is protected from water in case it gets knocked off the deck. If it does get knocked off it could still go to the bottom if it is not a floating unit so a leash or float of some kind will not only help keep it dry, but you'll be able to get it back.

GOING TO WHERE THE FISH ARE

Choosing the Right Boat to Get You There

There are two questions that should be considered when choosing the right boat: "What will be the fishing for?" and "where will the fishing activities be?" Always look for the signs of quality check the carpet and the compartments - they could be plastic, metal or fiberglass. Look at the little but very important things like the 1000 GPH bilge pump, the six gauge wiring instead of ten or eight that is because heavier wires gives more power from the battery up to the trolling motor.

There is Five Star Advantage that ranger dealers often speak to their customers: Quality, safety, innovation, performance, and value. Below is a list of "must have" things when buying your first boat.

Tow Vehicle - This is one of the most important pieces of your equipment, ensure that it has the rating to get the job done like loading up to 3500 lbs. of weight that could easily pull the boat up the hills and mountainous treks. More than likely, your best bet will be a pick-up truck, with the proper towing package.

Bass Boats - For first timers, consider a second hand boat. This will be a trial and error stage where fishing skills can be tested. Consider a larger boat, which is about 19 feet with an engine that can produce 20 to 30 mph speeds for larger bodies of water should you need it.

Aluminum - In smaller lakes, a 16-18 foot aluminum boat is a good choice. It is cheaper than fiberglass and more forgiving of bangs, running up into shallows and hitting stumps and rocks. The only downside is that it rides rougher even with the slightest winds.

Fiberglass - This type of boat with a two-stroke engine is much more expensive which could cost from $20,000 to as much as $50,000. The good thing with this boat is that it could handle bigger, rougher water and still give you a smooth ride.

Brand new versus second hand. Buying a second hand boat is not only cheaper but holds their value longer and better. The downside is that you'll probably inherit someone else's troubles. During casual inspection, outboard engine problems are not easily identified. The best thing to do is bring someone you trust with you to inspect a prospective boat or buy from someone you know instead.

Handling the boat. Listen to the pitch change when trimming down. Although it will be very difficult for beginners like trying to launch and retrieve the boat backing it down the ramp. Never worry, because everyone passed that stage and there are not many boat owners that are not willing to help a first timer learn. Sometimes all it takes is just 4 or 5 hours to learn the basics.

Buying a dreamboat is very exciting. It is not the boat that really matters but the experiences that come with fishing.

To make the activity easier for the first timers, here is a list of tips that you can use when choosing an ideal fishing boat.

1. It is important to consider the purpose of the fishing boat.

Buying a fishing boat has one main purpose, to be used in fishing. However, before choosing the perfect fishing boat, it is important to consider all the other purposes.

First, the place where the fishing boat will be used should be taken into account. Will it be in some saltwater, in rocky rivers, or in other bodies of water like lakes?

Will it be long runs to get to your destinations? Do you need 150 HP to get you there?

2. The budget

When buying a fishing boat, it is important to know if the buyer can afford to acquire a boat. Fishing boats, or any boat for that matter, can be very expensive. Hence, the buyer should know how far his budget would go as far as fishing boat prices are concerned.

3. The warranties

It is extremely important to know if the fishing boat has a warranty. It should be analyzed and meticulously scrutinized because not all warranties are created equal.

Hence, it is best to buy a fishing boat from dealers that will provide the necessary services in case their product is found to be defective.

4. The certification

When buying a fishing boat, it is important to take note if it is certified by the "National Marine Manufacturers Association" or the NMMA. This agency guarantees that the certification they give to every boat manufacturer is a guarantee that the fishing boat had passed the agency's standard of excellence.

The bottom line is that, people should do more than just look around when choosing the ideal fishing boat. They should learn how to look for the important details in order to ensure that the boat they have acquired is definitely worth their money.

You can browse around for boats and accessories in your area at iboats. http://bit.ly/2bjevJh

Going to the Fish

If you were told that there is one particular species of fish that most would describe as tough, smart, outwitting, and elusively hard to catch, then it's the bass, in all its shapes, sizes, and sub-classes. Bass are fighters, they are ever elusive, a predator by nature, and prized catch, of many an aspiring angler.

You can catch fish, bigger fish, more often, and in more places by having a proactive plan and approach, stacking the odds in your favor of success. Catching more fish and enjoying the process, is what this basic guide is all about.

The hunter becomes the hunted. A small change in your thinking and approach can lead to angling success. Start thinking like the watery hunter. Understand the bass as a hunter and opportunist. Observe, learn, follow, study, and use its natural habits, preferences, patterns, habits, and prey, in your angling strategy. You will have some interesting fish tales to tell. And you may even learn something from the ones that get away.

It's true, no matter what the context, body of water, situation or condition, regardless of secrets, tips, science, or techniques, bass fishing is challenging and rewarding at the same time. To ensure hours of countless pleasure, follow the pointers provided here for fishing and always be anticipating the next bite.

There are various aspects, working in combination in the art, science, and sport that is fishing. Strategy and synergy, contribute to eventual consistent and repeatable success. Equipment, location, lures, dawn and or dusk, shallow or deep waters, it does not matter. There are techniques for each of them.

Novices, beginners, seasonal and seasoned anglers alike, are all welcome to flip through these pages to discover some sought after truths about bass fishing. In the end, it is as much about the process, enjoyment, and appreciation, as it is about the fish.

Become an observant, student of nature, itself. Begin to understand the fish's habits and patterns. Do so using all to your advantage as you undertake your own journey.

Bass are by far the most widely distributed fish in North America. Bass are within easy reach for most (within 1 days' travel at most), largemouths, smallmouths, spotted, all await.

Various scientists have shown that bass almost calculate the amount of energy it will take them to go after the prey vs. the return. If this is true and verified, what are the implications for us anglers? Outsmarting them, of course! It's all in the basics, the strategies, battle plan, tease, and techniques we choose to use in this process. This will dictate and determine our success.

It is said that 90% of the fish are in 10% of the water. Going out onto a body of water and blindly casting probably isn't going to be successful. Sure, you'll get lucky by random chance a few times, but it would be much better to get, at least, some idea of where to go where fish might be *likely* to be. How can you know this if you've never been to an area before or are new to it?

Weedy, shallow bays, hard-bottom flats, rocks, trees and or other structures, creek, channels, deeper waters, drops, bluffs and more can all be part of their moving patterns and habitat throughout the year and where they look for food. They also like being close to access point to deeper water. More later on their preferred spots and how to optimize these patterns.

Nothing could be said here that will be correct 100% of the time given the vast area and bodies of water we all will be fishing. Read up or watch videos on the local area you'll be fishing. When I've looked for new places to fish, not only did I want to know where to put my boat in, but I wanted to know what kind of fish are there, which way to go, what techniques/lures to use, and what spots to fish specifically. Through several articles and a couple of Youtube videos, I was able to get a pretty good idea of the strategy I was going to employ when I got there. This can allow you to get a leg up knowledge wise without having to go out and learn it all from scratch aimlessly by yourself.

If you're lacking information, you can gather it yourself. Usually, the night before a trip, as you're getting lures and rods ready, or maybe filling a float plan, you can spend about 20 or 30 mins checking out the maps. Google, Yahoo, Bing, and MapQuest all offer aerial view map features that just might clue you into good spots to fish like points, humps, deep holes, channels, docks, or subsurface structure or cover.

You can use the road map feature to find routes to your launch sites and park land shown in green. And you can use the satellite feature to determine the good areas near banks, on points, or subsurface to find fish.

https://www.google.com/maps

Know your area as best you can *before* you go. That's the best and quickest way to at least end up in the vicinity of where fish might be that day. Look for any irregularities from rock piles, to ledges, to other man-made structures. Fish will usually relate to those things through most of the year. Look for spawning fish in shallows in the Spring. Fish do move from time to time and throughout the day according to conditions. Locating them is the first step. From there, you can start your patterning of the fish for that day.

LURE NOISE

Do everything you can to trigger their feeding response and ensure a strike. Often though, you'll want to make your lures and tackle are as quiet as possible. More times than not, I'm looking for relatively quiet baits. That's a hard thing since it seems like every bait on the market these days has a rattle in it. But, certain times, you will want noise. If I do want noise, I prefer the deeper, more hollow sound some lures have. Something like what is called a "one knocker" emits. The sound of 25 BB's inside of something like a Rat-L-Trap just hasn't inspired as much confidence in me. I have caught fish on them, but I don't think it was largely due to that sound in particular, and may have been in spite of it.

I'm much more in favor of baits that create a good water disturbance like paddle tail swimbaits, large single Colorado blade spinner baits, or wide wobble crankbaits. To me, it seems the fish respond more to that than noise when sight is hindered in less clear water for them. I fished a two day float trip down the Potomac river with my brother one time and caught all kinds of smallmouth on four inch, minnow profile, paddle tail swimbaits in water that looked like chocolate milk. We rigged them with nothing, but a 1/8 oz. jig head.

Also, remember, fish are a lot like you, on hot, humid days, they look for shelter, food, and comfort. These are their hideout and feeding ground (no different than us, wanting to sit under an umbrella, or in front of the TV, in an air-conditioned environment, trying to stay cool and enjoy our snack-foods). Knowing and considering these habits, will help you catch more fish. Look for the lily pads, think cover, giving them shade from the sun. Find the right depth, structure, and hide-away (they normally look for cover, like any other predator) and their lightning-fast speed enabled them to cover water quickly and really strike and attack their prey.

It isn't always the lure that makes the noise. In fact, that's part of the function of a Carolina rig. The subtle clacking or clicking noise made by the weight and the bead hitting together is said to be an attractor. If I do prefer noise, I prefer it to be subtle like this too. It's higher pitch, but not quite so in your face producing a loud racket. I especially like this with crawfish baits as that could resemble some of the noise their hard shelled bodies make coming into contact with itself, food, and the rocky environment surrounding them.

There are also a number of add on small bead rattles that can be inserted into soft plastics or slipped on with a rubber harness to a jig. Here again, I think this is a good imitator if jig fishing the bottom to resemble crawfish forage.

WHAT'S THE BEST LURE COLOR?

I think fishermen are perpetually on the quest for lures with a color that "works". At best I would say, it depends. But, mostly, I think the best color is natural. Or maybe even none. Sometimes, I believe movement may play a bigger role rather than lure color or even shape necessarily. For example, in low visibility conditions, fish may be more likely to rely on their lateral line sense rather than sight. In which case, you'd need something that resembles distressed forage in the water causing the right kind of disturbance.

If I had to choose a color, as close to natural as is possible is what I choose. For example, a pumpkinseed senko is pretty damn close to a big thick night crawler in the water. Or a natural colored swimbait or hard crankbait like a Rapala. Not that I'll never use other colors, sometimes, I use some with blood marks or red hooks (again for realism). And in stained water if I really want the fish to try to see the lure, I'll go with chartreuse (or if trying to get a reaction bite) if nothing else is working. An exception to this rule may be where I use black, black/blue, or smoke colored worms. We seem to have success with these particularly in the Potomac river. My only guess as to why is that the fish can see the silhouette of the lure better. They can definitely see it in mid water, but more importantly on the sandy river bottom which is very similar to pumpkinseed color. If I can make my bait stand out visually like that, I'll try it. It's been particularly important this year as the water has not been clear all year.

There are many things in the sport of fishing that make absolutely no sense at all. Much is done out of superstition or tradition. Some baits don't even look anything like what a fish would eat. Who came up with those things? I prefer not to go that route. Let's take a logical approach to this and control everything we can control in a tough sport. I remember reading a while back in Field and Stream magazine, I believe, that they actually tested bait colors on a tank full of bass. They used the original Rapala hard crankbait pattern in many different colors. There was mechanical arm that pulled the lures around the tank and they recorded the frequency with which the bass bit each color. The natural color (white/silver bottom and black top) got bit FAR MORE FREQUENTLY. Something like a factor of 10:1 even with all of those other lures of the same design, but different color in the water at the same time.

This is a logical approach especially in unfamiliar places. In fly fishing, we call it "matching the hatch" or trying to use the fly that looks most like what the fish are foraging for. In freshwater fishing, this is not always the approach. I almost always take a match the hatch approach to freshwater fishing. It's better than going about it blindly or in a superstitious fashion. I use natural, real-looking bait as the first step in my pattern development that day. But, sometimes, it is the fact that a bass sees something different that it isn't accustomed to that triggers the bite. This may especially be true in highly pressured areas. But, more often than not, I'm going with realistic looking lures.

I do like the color red or orange shades fading into red in some crawfish crankbaits. It's also really important to remember that what you see above the water is not what is reality below the water. Red is one of those colors. It is absorbed by the water depth very quickly. So any bright red you see on the bait in your hand will be significantly reduced at any depth.

Additionally, here is one of the things I didn't understand about chartreuse baits for the longest time. I thought it was just supposed to be a neon color that nearly anything underwater could see. And some may use it for that. But, here's what I think its real value is. Baits with chartreuse highlights, like soft plastics with the tips colored, can mimic the brightly yellow colored fin tips in bait fish. I didn't realize this being a real benefit until I watched a guy dip soft plastics in dye. He used a plain white fluke soft plastic and Spike it dye. Even in his clear water swimming pool, the fin tips became highlighted and looked a lot like the baitfish in this picture below. In that sense, chartreuse highlighted baits could reflect the patterns of baitfish more accurately.

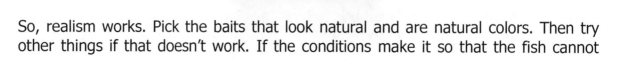

So, realism works. Pick the baits that look natural and are natural colors. Then try other things if that doesn't work. If the conditions make it so that the fish cannot see very well as in stained or muddy water, black lures can stand out better. Sunny days may be best for reflecting shiny metal spoon flashes of gold and silver. On cloudy days, you may find that the UV light getting through makes fluorescent colored lures like chartreuse stand out more. Let the conditions dictate your choices on any given day. And remember, locating the fish first is of the utmost importance. Lure choice is always second to that.

LURE SCENT

Most freshwater fishing lures probably don't have scent impregnated into them. Any type of hard bait such as a crankbait or spoon surely doesn't, at least not yet. However, there are a number of soft plastics that have scent impregnated into them. Scents from garlic, to anise, to coffee have all been used.

I imagine not every scent works to entice fish to bite, but the more common ones like Berkley's Powerbait scent and Coffee Tubes I don't think are ever a detriment. Other variables in fishing can be a detriment on certain days and certain conditions. In my experience, scent isn't one of them.

One of my fishing partners used to use a line of soft plastics made locally. The maker would load up on a unique scent in these lures. There were many times we'd go smallmouth bass fishing in the river and he'd use one of the crawfish soft plastics. The smallmouth would pick off the crawfish claws and legs until nothing was left, but the body mass. My partner would keep it rigged and just keep fishing it and he'd still be able to catch a few more fish on it even though it didn't look like anything now except for a mangled piece of plastic. I believe it was due to the strong scent that remaining plastic still held.

Scent is probably best used on slower moving baits. Fast moving baits may go by a fish so fast the scent may not play a role in the strike. I'm not sure. But, in any case, you can use them to get the fish to hold on just a little longer if you're dealing with finicky fish on a particular day.

You'll most often see scented baits in grub, worm, and tube patterns. But, other patterns could be scented as well. You can make and mold your own and buy scent additives. Scents also come in dips, dyes, markers, liquid potions, and wand type applicators you can use to apply scents to non-scented plastics.

Generally, I keep a few scented baits on hand all the time and have scent applicators ready to go in my PFD pockets for non-scented baits.

WATER, WEATHER, TIMING, AND OTHER ENVIRONMENTAL ASPECTS

As mentioned throughout this text so far, there are numerous factors that we often do not consider, and or dismiss, when we first start out, fishing. These would include consideration of:

Water stratification and depths (bass are found at varying levels and knowing where (at which level), to fish for them is paramount); shallow or deep, sometimes both.

As far as water temperatures goes, during a yearly/seasonal cycle, waters move, turn and gets re-oxygenized. As temperatures fall, from deep below and throughout ice forms, floats to the surface, melts and moves down again. Science has provided us with enough evidence that THREE distinct layers form in a body of water, say a lake for example. Deeper/colder, Middle-ground/milder transitional layer and the top/surface/warmer waters. Heeding these levels and varying temperatures, and looking oxygen-rich spots are all factors to consider even before heading out. Think the process through. Think like the fish would. Ask yourself, where would you go in all likelihood, if you were faced with the same situation. The answer will mostly lead you to where the fish most likely are.

A temperature gauge and depth meter can all prepare you better, as an angler, knowledgeable and prepared, to assess the environment, better understand it, learn from it, and use the information you gather and have on hand, due to these readings and instruments, to KNOW or best judge, where the fish will be at! Depth is a great indicator of what the bass are up to and where they will be most likely found. This will dictate your approach, tackle and how you execute your angling skills to land your next fish.

If you fish at the right level, understanding why the fish are there, on the move, feeding, and more, you will increase your odds drastically of getting strikes and hooking your next big catch. It might even be a trophy. The depth is usually related to water temperature and the optimal comfort zone of the bass. Always ask yourself, what they would prefer on a day like today and then go fish there. Measure with temperature, depth sensors, and GPS to establish the pattern and depth of the day.

Temperature: Optimal and Changing

Most bass species prefer a temperate climate. Their metabolism is influenced, if not governed pretty much by the surrounding waters they find themselves in. They can also tolerate quite a wide range of temperatures, therefore, we can fish pretty much throughout the year. It is also less widely known that ice-fishermen hook bass at around 32-39.2 degree water temperatures, in deeper waters. When it does get colder, they get somewhat more sluggish, as their environment cools down significantly and bearing this in mind will yield and improve your catch.

Oxygen is also very important to fish. The hotter it gets, the closer they will stay to shore, and to plant-life, which produces oxygen and or where they might catch the occasional breeze. Reading these signals nature provides right, will prepare any angler better to go where the fish are and hook your next big one. Also look for spots that are not too stagnant and filled with decaying plants, as this might be an oxygen-deprived area with not a large concentration of fish. They need to "breathe" to stay alive too.

Water Conditions: Clarity

Clear and or murky, you will find fish in both. Their behavior and mode of attack will change as they plan how to best expend their energy in the hunt for food and survival. Predators by design, they prefer cover and structure and deeper waters. When spawning, or on very hot days, you may be most likely, find them more in the shallows.

Bass almost always have a back door access to deeper waters. These facts should be able to point you in the general vicinity of where the fish are quite well. The male bass is also very protective of the nest/spawn site and will defend it, strike at any perceived threat or intruder. Fishing is no longer left up to random trial and error casting. Now, today, replaced with a more driven, focused, thought-through, analytical, and competitive approach. We try to understand habits, patterns, environment, conditions, and time of year, at times relying on the aid of technology and devices to assist and better your chances of finding and hooking the fish successfully. If the waters are clear, head for deeper waters as a general rule of thumb.

Noise/Disturbances/Vibrations

DO NOT DISTURB signs are hard to post in the water! Always remember that there is some truth to not chasing the fish away and being somewhat careful and quiet around them. The bass particularly uses its whole body as a sounding board. Any surface disturbance, water movement and or displacement will attract their attention. This can, in fact, both help or hurt your angling hopes.

Paddles hitting kayak hulls, noisy shuffling of equipment, and even the sound of a fast, far cast may interfere and or get their attention. Being aware of any, movement, spotting fish bolting off in one direction can be a good indicator that you spooked them. Wearing a good pair of polarized sunglasses may also help you see better in the bright sunlight and glare. Reflections off the surface of the water is diminished allowing your vision to penetrate farther.

Also, keep in mind that due to the refraction caused by the surface of the water, fish can often see you before you see them. It's wise to approach a likely area and keep your distance at first. As you move closer, certainly try to keep a low profile and don't alert them that you're there.

Color, Sunlight, Time of Day

Most bass anglers propose dawn and dusk to be the best feeding time for the bass, not the height of day or when the sun is at it brightest and the water maybe a degree or two too warm and they head for the deep and or cover. It is a matter of appealing to their natural instincts.

They are keen observers. Movement and color have been researched in the bass species. Picking presentations of baits, lures that closest resemble live bait or resembles their prey will maximize your chances of catching more bass. This does not mean that they will not strike at night for example or at other times during the day, you might just have to adapt and use some specialist techniques to lure them out of hiding a bit more.

Time of Year: Seasons and Things Changing

Surroundings, weather and angling rules change and keep changing. The stage and players do not remain the same and even on the same day, day to day, things will vary. This variety is what keeps most of us guessing, adapting, changing strategy, bait, depth etc. all in the continued hope and pursuit of catching your next big one.

As to the best time to catch bass, opinions vary greatly on this topic. In some areas, fishing is only allowed after spawning. Spring, Summer, and Fall (with Fall being the best for most bigger fish) and even Winter some form of bass fishing is available to you, depending on where you are, what the weather conditions are like, and what type of year the bass are having (spawning success, health of the body of water they live and thrive in, the eco-system, stocking, pollution etc.)

As pointed out earlier, weather affects behavior. The season and type of water, might all require different approaches, equipment, and lure presentations.

As an angler, this will not phase you in any way. On the contrary, it provides you with the opportunity to shift gears, change strategy, tools, refine skills, and learn more about your opponent and its habits. By being alert, aware, and observant, you will learn a lot about the fish. It is no longer a passive sport. Windy, low or high air pressure, water temperature, choppy waves and surface movement of the water, cloudy skies, with lots of cloud cover, masking the sun, could dictate whether fish will be biting or not. Color of plastic worms might be adjusted from pumpkinseed (on bright days), to white on cloudy days with not a lot of sun around. Modifying your fishing techniques and adapting to weather patterns, even adjusting your bait/lures, strategy, all bear witness of an alert bass master!

Bass are also sensitive to very bright sunlight, so then you might find them looking for some shady cover and or cooler waters. That knowledge will prepare you well for where to go and look for them. Increasing your odds of finding them.

Predatory Nature and Creatures of Habit: What the Fish Tell Us

There predators of the deep are rich in their life cycles, habits and patters. It is their nature after all. They are somewhat predictable. As hunters, they do certain things, instinctively and, as anglers, we capitalize on it. There are lots of facts about the species worth knowing and key to understanding the secret to unlocking the success of bass fishing. Thinking like a hunter, ourselves, and at times like the fish, can increase your odds and success significantly.

Being one with nature and its intricate patterns and balance allow fisherman to be skilled, precise, well prepared, and more successful, rather than leaving it up to luck or random chance to secure a bite.

Preferred Habitat and Fishing Structures

One author likens contour and topographic maps to bass fishermen, like treasure maps to pirates once were. Lines show elevation, depth etc. Get an idea of what the bottom of the body of water (like a lake for instance) would look like. It is rarely flat, often characterized by rises and humps, slopes, channels, and drop-offs.

Slopes and access points into deeper water should also yield more frequent, larger hauls, and more strikes, as bass prefer to have access to deeper waters and are often on the move, hunting and feeding and or defending territory.

SELF-CONFIDENCE

The belief in your ability to locate and catch the various bass species, is by far the best tool of the trade to foster and develop over time. This cannot be purchased and is the personal call to every fisherman, to include in his/her tackle-box. There have been many times, I've tied on a favorite bait and felt like I almost tricked a bass into biting with my mind.

Whether you choose to use spinners, or swear by plastic worms, crawfish, or have a favorite lure for reasons that are your very own, you use what works the best and what you believe will produce the fish you want. Positive attitude goes a long way when learning how to fish for bass and other freshwater species. Profiting from ongoing experience, success, and failure, your angling odds will keep improving. Practice in this case, will go a long way to enable success in this unpredictable, varying situation when you are one-on-one with some of the most popular game and sporting fish.

After all of my experience, I feel, on most days, no matter what, I can go out there and have a really good expectation of adapting to the conditions and get at least one fish to bite. Everyone gets skunked every now and then, but those days are fewer and fewer the more you learn and the more time you put into the pursuit. If it wasn't a challenge, it wouldn't be fun.

Conversely, it's easy to have a bad day and let the negativity perpetuate itself in your mind. If you think there are no fish, there probably won't be any fish. Try to assume the attitude that no matter what, you can use your knowledge and experience and try to piece something together despite the conditions that are hampering your efforts.

KNOTS FOR FISHING

There are many different knots that you can use to tie your lines. Any one of them will work just fine. Some are better suited to certain instances than others. Which one you choose is a matter of personal preference. It is important that you tie the knot correctly and secure it properly. Failing to do so will result in lost fish and a lot of frustration.

Before you tighten a knot, you should wet it either with saliva or by dipping it in water. This will help the knot slide and seat properly. Lubrication also decreases excessive heat which dramatically weakens monofilament. Heat is generated by the friction created when knots are drawn up tight.

Seating the knot means to tie it tightly. Tighten knots with a steady, continuous pull. Make sure the knot is tight and secure. After it is tied, pull on the line and leader to make sure it holds. It is better to test it now than when a fish is on.

You will also need to trim the ends neatly. Use nippers to trim the material as close as possible without nicking or damaging the knot.

Here are a few of the more common knots you can try:

Arbor Knot (Backing To Reel)

Step 1: Wrap the line around the arbor of your spool and tie an overhand knot around the standing line.

Step 2: Tie a second overhand knot on the tag end a few inches from the first.

Step 3: Moisten the line and the two overhand knots. Tighten the smaller knot and holding the spool in your left-hand pull on the standing line with your right hand sliding the first overhand knot against the arbor of the spool. The second overhand knot will keep this from slipping. Trim the tag end.

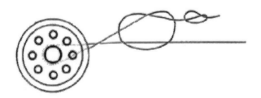

Albright

The Albright knot is used in situations where you need to join two lines of greatly unequal diameter or of different material. You can also use this knot for joining of main line to backing material or main line to leader.

Step 1: Loop the heavier line (wider diameter) and place it between your thumb and index finger of your left hand. Pass the lighter line through the formed loop leaving about 8 inches. Pinch the lighter line in with the line already in your left hand. (See illustration 1)

Step 2: Make approximately 10 wraps with the lighter line wrapping away from you and working from left to right. With each wrap, work your thumb and index finger along holding these wraps in place, trying not to let up any pressure on your left hand. On the 10th wrap, come around and then through the remaining loop.

Take the standing line in your right hand and pull gently as you push the wraps with your left hand towards the closed loop. Alternate between the end of the lighter line and on the standing part until the wraps are against the tag end. Make sure the wraps do not go over each other and that you don't push them too far. Pull the tag tight then pull on the standing part of both lines until the knot is secure.

Step 3: Finally, clip the two short pieces close to the knot.

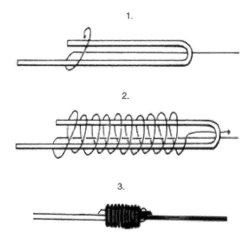

Blood Knot (Monofilament to Monofilament)

The blood knot is a knot used for attaching two pieces of monofilament together, primarily for rebuilding tapered leaders. This is an extremely strong knot when formed properly and should be tied with monofilament close in diameter. Best use is for monofilament 10 lbs. and up.

Step 1: Lay both sections of monofilament across one another. Wrap one section 5-6 times around the other bringing the end back down through the loop formed by both. (See illustration 1)

Step 2: Wrap the other line 5-6 times around the remaining portion of the first line and pass it's free end up through the formed loop. (See illustration 2)

Step 3: Moisten the knot with your mouth, and while holding the long ends pull the knot tight. Clip the short ends close and the knot is complete.

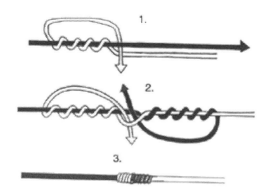

Improved Clinch Knot (Leader to lure)

The Improved Clinch knot is used for fastening the leader to the lure. If you are using over 12 Lb. test line, this is not a recommended knot.

Step 1: Thread your leader tippet through the eye of the hook. Wrap the end of the leader around the standing line 5 times for lines up to eight pound test and four times for lines from 8-12lb test. (You can also turn the hook 5 or 4 times).

Step 2: Take the tag end of the leader and pass it through the gap between the eye of the hook and the first wrap. Continue the tag end back up through the main loop just formed.

Step 3: Moisten the knot with your mouth, and while holding the hook in your left-hand pull on the standing leader allowing the knot to seat tightly against the hook. Clip the excess line.

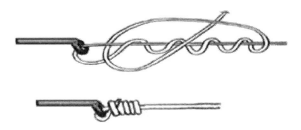

Surgeon's Knot

The Surgeon's Knot is a knot also used for attaching two pieces of monofilament together or braid to mono or fluoro. It is a very fast and easy knot to tie and is usually preferred more than the blood knot. This is a great knot for joining two pieces of monofilament that are greatly different in diameter. When you are building a leader, tied correctly, this knot is generally stronger than the blood knot. This is a very quick and easy knot for attaching lines together in heavy wind where more complicated knots may be more difficult to tie.. You can do this one in the dark.

Step 1: The main line should come in from the left and the line to be attached should come from the right. Overlap the two pieces approximately 6 or so inches. (See illustration   1)

Step 2: Pinch the overlapped lines together on the left between your thumb and index finger. Do the same with the sections on the right and make a loop by crossing it over itself. Take the long and short lines that are in your right hand and pass them through the formed loop, around, and back through a second time. (See illustration 2)

Step 3: Pull both pieces being held in each hand away from each other closing the knot. Moisten and pull tight. Once this not is secure you can tighten it further by pulling individual pieces. I would not recommend this knot for line over 30lbs because it will be hard to tighten and the strength of the knot will only be there if tightened all the way.

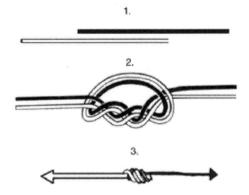

These are only a few of the knots you can use to tie your lines. Ask others what they prefer and learn from your fishing buddies if you want. There are all sorts of knots and no one is perfect. As we've said, it's a matter of personal preference.

TECHNIQUES FOR BASS FISHING

The Art of Accurate Casting

Mastering basic casting is key. Most spinning and bait casting reel and rod combinations today, are made for hassle-free, ease-of-use flexibility by a variety of anglers at multiple levels of proficiency.

Try to eliminate errors from your basic style and technique. Skill and accuracy should matter more than strength and it is not always about getting it as far out, as fast as you possibly can although this might be important in certain situations and circumstances.

Accurate casting with artificial lures is paramount. You already have something fake on the line. You want to make what we call the best presentation possible. This isn't like casting a stinky bait out or a live bait struggling on the line and, essentially calling in fish from miles around. Casting, getting your hook and line into the water, at the exact right depth, imitating prey, and doing so with extreme, pin-point accuracy, is what this is all about. Hitting your target with confidence is a very basic skill to master and refine. Getting the hook out to exactly where you wanted it to be is what you should practice and work toward.

Casting is one part of this process. Getting the lure to the right depth quite another. Advanced bass anglers suggest using a countdown or counting method. Quite simple really. Get an idea of how fast your bait sinks in the water. If it is a soft plastic with a ¼ oz. bullet weight on it, it will sink fast. If it is a slow sinking crankbait, it will sink slowly. Either way, do it at the side of the boat or in the shallows to see how fast that particular bait sinks. From the moment the bait hits the water, start counting, 1000, 1000 and 1, 1000 and 2, 1000 and 3, estimating the seconds it will take for it to drop in the water. This will help you know better what you are doing or when it hits the bottom, for example. Whether or not it got caught on something in the process or there is a change in depth or contour there. You establish reference points for yourself on and in the water for subsequent casts and future trips to this same location.

Hands-on and rod in-hand time is the best way to practice. Practice-plugs in the park, or your own backyard on dry land, will make you that much more effective and accurate, no matter what the body of water, or style of fishing you choose to pursue. Whether spinning, bait casing or fly fishing, there is something for everyone to learn. Even missed targets, attempts and failure, are also good teachers, as this is somewhat of a routine you can master and learn.

Casting a lure with a spinning reel and bait casting are very similar with some notable exceptions. Lure fishing, spinning, spoons, plugs, top water lures, crankbaits, trolling are all basic techniques that require exposure, quick demos, and hands-on practice. **We highly suggest a video, DVD, or online in-depth explanation and learning.** Watching a fishing show or two, and getting pointers from other anglers and professionals, as well as finding and defining your own style that you are comfortable and successful with. The beauty of bass fishing, is that it offers something for everyone, no matter what your prior experience with fishing might be. The more you learn, the more you realize how much more you still have to learn and don't know.

Focusing on your grip for both spinning reels and bait casters, concentrating on rod swing timing, angle of release, picking a target, aiming to land your lure in the middle of that target, is a good approach. As a general rule of thumb, a good arc in the air as a travel path en route to the water, is a good reference and goals to have, as you set out to improve your casting technique and accuracy. On non-windy days, that high arc is fine. If you're casting into the wind or have a cross wind, a side arm cast, more like a line drive, closer to the water's surface may yield more accuracy.

Line control is crucial to avoid overshooting, get a gentler landing, slow flight (by touching the spool with the tip of your thumb (also known to anglers as "feathering") is useful. You can do something similar even with a spinning reel by letting the line shoot through your fingers on your left hand to slow the descent of the lure or stop it altogether. I especially use the stop it altogether technique if I know I have overshot mid-cast.

Advancing further, you'll learn to recognize the effect that cross wind has on lure flight as well as the different effects on each type of line you choose. Braided lines are more subject to catching wind than mono and fluoro. Mono and braid also float. Fluorocarbon does not. This may play a slight role in how your lure is presented as it enters the water, especially moving water. Mending is something we often talk about in fly fishing, but can be used with other lines like braid too especially in moving water. If you sit on a body of water and have cross wind or current running down stream and you cast upstream to drift a lure down, what will happen? The lure will go with the current probably. If you have it weighted significantly, it may stay relatively still, but the line on the surface of the water will still move. It will develop a big bow in the line. This may affect the presentation of the lure because it's changing the direction you're retrieving it from. It might also change the depth and lift it up. Something similar may happen if you make a cast straight across with a high arc, but have a strong cross wind. The lure may make your target, but the line will be bowed out again. To correct this, you can mend your line. To do so, reel up any slack, and simply lift a large portion of your line off the water and move your rod tip over laying the line back on the water more in line with your lure's position out there. You can repeat this a few times as your lure drifts down a section of river. If the wind is too strong, a mend still may not work. In that case, you may need to re-position yourself or your boat to make up for the cross wind.

Although, there are some last thoughts we can offer on some of the more common casting mistakes. These errors are well-documented in existing literature and easily overcome, to optimize your bass fishing experience. Here are but a few issues most beginners struggle with:

1. Overshot lure with too much power in the initial cast and the line release not slowed.
2. The lure falling short or being too light, with the line being released too early during the cast and or the rod held too high after the line was released.
3. The lure landing too hard, due to the release at too low of an angle and not arcing enough in the air.
4. Inaccurate casting (the most common). Missing the mark, where the lure goes off-course with too much side-to-side action/motioning of the rod while casting. Practicing reel and line control, as well as the overhead cast might help.

Lots of texts suggest thinking of casting, compared to the movement of the arms on a clock-face, beginning in the two o'clock position, coming back to around the ten o'clock position with the rod slightly lowered as the lure drops deeper into the water. For most beginners this visualization often helps refine technique. But, remember, casts will not always be directly overhead. You may have sidearm or other type of casts in your arsenal in order to get the bait where you want it.

Casting a Baitcaster Reel

Things are slightly different when using a baitcaster reel and rod combo. If you're used to making long casts with light lures with spinning gear, you may get a few backlashes at first on a baitcaster. That's because, with a baitcaster, the fundamental difference is that it is a long smooth acceleration without a sudden stop, whipping of the rod, or flicking of the rod tip. What causes a backlash is the underlying layers of line accelerating on the turning spool faster than the above line going out. That last flick or whip of a rod tip that normally sends a small lure flying with spinning gear, actually accelerates a baitcaster spool too quickly causing the backlash. This can be mitigated by having your settings right. Let's go over how to get ready to cast a baitcast reel.

Many people say to use braid. You can use whatever line type you prefer. But, to start I prefer regular mono. It's a lot harder to untangle braid than mono when you're first practicing.

An important note here is that you must use heavier gear with baitcasters. You're not going to be throwing 1/16 oz. jig heads. Start off with no lighter than 12 pound mono. More reasonably, try something like 20 pound mono to develop the skill. Tie on at least a ¼ oz. lure. Something with a slim profile so your first few casts aren't stopped by wind resistance.

You'll need to set two different settings. Your magnetic or centrifugal brakes which will be some kind of dial or a plate on the side of the reel to pop off and move the pieces on pins out. You'll also need to set your cast control knob.

Both of these setting can be set relatively high to start so that you can get the feel of how the mechanisms should work. You can set the brakes, if you have a dial, anywhere from 5 – 10. Or half to all of the pins internally if you have to open up to reach centrifugal brakes. This setting mainly attempts to slow a rapid acceleration down so as not to backlash. A higher setting takes less skill to control and a lower setting takes more skill to control. Start with a higher setting to learn.

Next you have the cast control knob, probably next to your drag wheel setting and reel handle. This is a friction device only. It lets the reel spool spin more or less freely depending on how tight you set it. How tight do you want it? A good rule of thumb to start with is to raise your rod tip up with the lure almost reeled into the tip top. Press your spool release button and adjust the knob looser until your lure just barely begins to descend. That's right about where you want it. You may note that each different lure may make these setting function differently especially if they are different weights. And you'd be right. Be sure to re-adjust if you change lures.

Making the cast. You can use a similar arc, either overhead or side arm, as you would with spinning gear, but again, be sure to make it more of a slower, sweeping movement without that sudden acceleration or flicking action. Let the heavier lure and action of the loaded rod do most of the work. You start by engaging the spool release button and keeping your thumb on the spool to prevent the lure from dropping. Go through your casting arc and release your thumb at about the 10 o'clock rod position to complete the cast. Be sure that immediately before or just as the lure hits the water, you put your thumb back on the spool. If you don't do this here, the lure hits the water and virtually stops, but the momentum is still carrying line off the spool turning relatively freely. It will start to exceed the speed of the now slowing line and cause a backlash if you don't manually stop it with your thumb.

Here's where the skill comes in. The lighter you set your settings, the more line will be allowed to come off the spool and the more distance you can get on a cast. But, you'll have to become quite adept at feathering the reel spool with your thumb tip. This will control the speed of the spool manually. It's a fine skill that takes a fair amount of practice. Get a Texas rigged worm with a large worm weight ahead of it. Go to the dock and start making a bunch of casts. Go for accuracy and skill in controlling the line.

After you have it down, begin to back off on your settings a little and increase your effort to thumb the reel properly. Allow yourself to make a few backlashes to get an idea of the end point so you can better control future casts. If you do backlash, the easiest way to get it out is to tighten your drag all the way down. Press your thumb hard on the spool covering as much surface area as possible. Crank the reel handle a few turns under the hard pressure of your thumb. This can help reposition some of the line layers so they can be pulled out. After a couple or a few turns, engage your spool release button and try to gently pull out the line. If you did it right, it should go right past where it was previously looped up in a tight tangle. If not, keep trying that until it does free. Pressure is what works here.

As you move into other types of casts like flipping and pitching, you may need to change your settings further. In something like a pitch, you may want to back off the friction on the cast control knob more towards free spool. You can still control with your thumb as line goes out, but keep your brakes high especially on a cast like this.

Continue to practice, get familiar with the settings and tuning of your reel and you'll pick up that fine motor skill in no time.

Set the Hook Quickly

This reduces the chances of the fish swallowing the bait and then needing the fisherman to perform minor surgery to get the hook out. If you do get a fish that is gut hooked, try to use a hook removal device like needle nose pliers or hemostats to help with the job. If it appears that you will have to do more harm than good to get the hook out just cut the line off as close to the hook as you can and hope for the best. In most instances the hook will work itself out and even if it doesn't the fish will have a better chance of living with the hook than if damage was done to his internal organs during the hook removal process. You can also use the through the gill hook removal technique to turn the hook over to remove with much success on bass.

Landing the Fish

Getting to know the feel of a fish on your hook, line and rod is very important. Retrieval is about more than simply getting the fish into your hands/net/boat. Mastery, maneuvering, responsiveness, knowledge of your tackle, well-balanced control, reel-clutching, fighting, arching/bending rods, and the various controls and settings, techniques. They are so much more than mere steps in a process and or sum-total of parts. To translate into a true blue-blood fishing experience and success, appreciation of the symphony of the interplay of processes is what is needed here. In essence, it's a sum of skills, but also an art form.

I often hear of fishing friends who went out for a day and hooked into several fish. What would otherwise be a decent catch number for a day of fishing turned out to be something like 8 bass hooked and 6 got away. That kind of sucks. What happened there? Likely a number of things. Getting a bite, hooking a fish, fighting the fish, and getting it in the boat are all different things and skills that will make for a successful day. Each phase of the process needs to be paid attention to and skillfully applied. Likely, these anglers did almost everything right and maybe got excited when bringing the fish into the boat. Now, we all know fish get away by not really being hooked or just mouthing a bait.

A bass' lips might as well be prehensile, meaning that they can function almost as good as a set of hands for a fish. I've seen bedding bass in crystal clear water grab my 6 hook crankbait and move it out of their nest with their lips going nowhere near the hooks. No matter how many times I tried to set it on them, they wouldn't get hooked. It's like you picking up broken sharp glass. If you're careful, you can do it quite easily without getting cut.

Back to the point, how can so many bass get off after you've surely hooked them securely? I've seen many anglers get excited at the instant a fish bites their lure, rightfully so, that's what we're in this sport for. But, the excitement can sometimes overrule concentration. An angler may make a big hook set and hold his rod high in the air while cranking the reel as fast as he can. What this does is bring the fish up to the surface where they can potentially head shake the hook loose. This is especially true with treble hooks on crankbaits. They can also jump and cause slack to get into the line loosening your hook. Lastly, if they are allowed to twist or rotate enough, they can use the leverage of the hook shank against the bait to pry their lips off the points. This all happens fast, but mechanically speaking, these are some of the common reasons so many fish get off in those last couple seconds before landing them.

Unless you're in a tournament, there's no need to rush it. You want to play the fish. Be sure of your hook set, if the fish shakes its head or goes on a run, let it, stop reeling, play the fish, adjust drag as needed, gain line when you can. Try to keep the fish down and prevent it from jumping. How do you do that with fishing line? You can't push him down. Sideways pressure on the fish works well for this, again, especially with treble hooks. Keeping your rod tip somewhat low and off at an angle to the side. As the fish runs laterally, you may need to switch sides quickly back the other direction for more side pressure and preventing the fish from coming up, jumping, or circling you. This is also more critical in shallows of lakes or a wide shallow river where you only have 3-5 feet of water column to keep the fish in. If you're reeling fish up from 25 or 30 feet, this will be less of an issue and you'll want to keep your rod tip up slightly.

There is nothing more exciting than a big fish on the run, apply pressure, keep the rod tip up slightly and increase or decrease the drag carefully, if required. You can easily fine tune drag mid-fight on spinning or casting reels. Watch tension and avoid line-breaks and allow the fish to tire.

Only attempt to bring the fish up when you've fought it for a sufficient amount of time and can either net or lip it quickly and land in the boat. When netting, try to net the fish from the head end, don't try to scoop it up from the tail.

Getting the fish close to you may require you to keep some of the line out from your rod tip and keeping your bail closed, holding the rod out and away from your body with your opposite hand so that you can lip the fish.

When lipping, grip the lower lip gently between your thumb and forefingers. It may help at this point to open your reel bail and lay your rod down. If the fish does shake free, it will go off without taking your rod with it, or worse, pulling a hook right into your skin. Unhook carefully or hold in the water while freeing it gently, but efficiently, without hurting the fish, adhering as close as possible, to current and accepted, catch-and-release practices.

Study after study has shown that the majority of fish species can survive being caught and released if they are handled and released properly. With most states now having laws requiring you to catch and release during some time of the year for some or most game species, there is a strong need to learn to release your catch in a way that will ensure its greatest chance of survival.

Here are some tips to help improve your fish's chance of survival once released back into the water.

Land your fish quickly if possible, but after sufficiently playing it out. The longer you fight the fish, the more energy the fish will use and will lesson his chance of survival. Also a weak and stressed fish is more vulnerable to predators and is also less able to fight off infection.

There is one exception to this and that is when you are fishing in very deep water. A fish caught in deep water needs time to adjust to the pressure changes as he is being reeled up to the boat or his air bladder will expand and he will not be able to swim back down to the deeper water.

Try to Reduce the Handling of the Fish

Leave the fish in the water as much as possible during the release phase. Use a hook removal tool if possible to reduce handling and don't let the fish thrash around and injure itself or someone else. If you must handle the fish try to use a wet towel or glove and return the fish to the water as soon as possible.

After the fish is unhooked you don't want to release him till he is strong enough to swim own his own. Hold the fish gently by its tail under water facing into the current. Move the fish gently back in forth till he can swim away on his own.

Practice catch and release whenever possible and remember the large fish don't taste any better than an average medium one if you plan to keep them. In many cases, some smaller fish may be better for eating than large ones. But, follow your state's size and creel limits. Generally, it's good to take a picture and let the hog's go back to catch again later unless you are the one actively managing a fishery.

HOW TO CATCH FISH IN WIND

High wind days can be aggravating for fishermen, but also good for fishing conditions. You just have to accept that it may ruin some of your finesse fishing techniques and you'll be fishing with things like search baits and power fishing most of the day.

I prefer to rig up spinner baits and crankbaits. Something a little on the heavier side so I can get it down if I need to fish deeper. It also allows me to get a really long cast so I can get a crankbait deeper. Use the wind as your friend or a tool in your favor. On the river, it may present a little more of a problem. You may have swirling or cross winds while you are trying to go downstream. But, chances are you can tuck away somewhere or use the bank of the river gorge to your advantage to better control your boat or to try other techniques you would like or think may be more successful that day. On rivers that meander, you'll likely have some parts of the day where the river gorge is not funneling the wind directly in your face. As you proceed through the meanders, you'll likely get a break from those conditions until you float back into the direction of the wind again. Maybe use that time to troll or just go right through it to a section where you know you can stop and fish in place with less direct wind.

You may have an upstream wind against a downstream current. This can present a good opportunity for trolling as well. You go upstream gently with the wind at your back assisting you. Your lure (I like to use 4" swimbaits for trolling) is slowly working its way upstream as you go. If your lure is heavy enough and your speed correct, you can keep a tight line and detect bites. This also works well with crankbaits to keep a tight line in high wind.

Often times, several factors will seem to be working against you in conjunction with each other. You may have an unpredictable swirling wind, but you can find a relatively shielded spot to park your yak. But, you're not within casting distance of your preferred hole or there is other grass or debris in the way. This can really limit your options that day. You may be stuck with only one or two techniques that you can work effectively. You may have to give up the big guys deep in that hole. Maybe there is a current seam between two islands you know little fish congregate in. You may end up with a day of numbers of little guys rather than going for big ones. That's still a fun day. Maybe you switch species all together. Maybe you know of one drop off on a leeward bank that holds rock bass and you fish for them for several hours in numbers.

In any case, try not to get frustrated. Try not to fight the conditions. Try to use the conditions to your advantage or at least stick to the ones that best suit the situation. You may be able to wait out some of those conditions like when the strong wind dies down toward the end of the day as the sun starts to go down in Summer. Be adaptable and have fun, but don't get frustrated. Take it as a challenge to enjoy and match your techniques to the conditions presented.

Whether you find yourself near shore, rocks, stream, river, lake, reservoir, or other body of water, strong rods, good hands, good tackle, appropriate preparation, can all make those fleeting moments of anticipation and elation at first strike momentous. The fights, flips, turns and jumps, attacks and hard hits, and landing of the fish, is what keeps us coming back.

Let us now turn to take a look at what other considerations, plan of attack, angling techniques, and specialty circumstances, can teach us about the enjoyable activity, that is fishing.

LURE TYPES

Fishing Artificial Baits

Spinning tackle and artificial baits and lures are increasing in popularity and the most popular form of fishing worldwide. As far as bass fishing is concerned, it is one of the easiest ways to attract fish, even for novices, and beginner anglers of all ages and fishing styles and skill-levels. Rotation, color and movement, staying as true as you can to the natural diet and target prey of the bass will optimize your chances. The shape and thickness of the spinning 'blade' on the lure affects the action and mobility of the lure. How it responds and acts in and under water.

Artificial lures can be utilized alone or in combination with live or natural baits. The size and type of lure will depend on the species, location, and style of fishing you prefer.

For bass fishing in particular, a couple of suggestions are to bear in mind that enticing the predators from below, takes skill, practice and patience. Having a handy pair of polarized sunglasses are a MUST! Keep on moving the bait around and play with the presentation through your list of techniques below. It is an art, acquired skill that gets better over time. When casting the bait out, try not to spook the fish, remembering that they are sensitive to sound, noise, movement, and vibrations. Being adaptable, switching baits, different color, different retrieves until you find the pattern that the fish like and are on at that time.

Hard Baits

Crankbaits

Plugs, surface lures, useful at all fishing levels, and at all speeds make these lures versatile, agile and an all-time favorite of many a bass angler. Matching the lure to the conditions you face, the circumstances, body of water, and specific species you are fishing for.

Mostly refers to lures, which are usually made from a variety of materials, including hard plastic or wood. With an added feature of a diving lip on the front (simulating effectively the movements of natural prey, wobbling, diving and swimming actions), entices the bass to strike. The rule of thumb, normally is that the larger the lip, the deeper it can dive. The angle and shape of the lip will matter too. You can go from a wake bait, which swims immediately subsurface to deep diving cranks that can go 25-30 feet down. Enhancements like rattles are also good for certain conditions. Some crankbaits float, others slowly sink, and others suspend. I find suspending or slow floating crankbaits to be more of what I prefer many times. If I pause the bait, I want it to stay in front of a potentially following fish, not immediately float or sink out of the strike zone.

You need a place to store your tackle and lures. The Plano waterproof storage boxes are the best.

http://bit.ly/2bHyN2V

The Koppers Livetarget crawfish crankbait is an excellent mid-level diver with realistic crawfish pattern painted on. I love this bait for river smallmouth action.

http://bit.ly/1SMALcS

The Strike King DVD Square Bill is a great shallow water crankbait good for getting a lot of deflection of rocks and structure with the square bill. Comes with that proven bait fish color pattern. I particularly like these for fishing shallow areas just off from banks.

http://bit.ly/1TRadMj

I like the Rapala Scatter Rap as a deep diving crankbait for use in deeper lakes or reservoirs. The relatively new scooped bills ad to the erratic action of the bait.

http://bit.ly/23ExaoI

Lipless Crankbait

Mostly referring to sinking-type lures, made from plastic, sometimes with many rattles inside for noise, , vibrations and causing disturbances underwater. Like the Rat-L-Trap I described earlier. These baits usually have a shad profile design to them and it is the shape of the body or the flattened head that gives it its action rather than an additional added plastic lip. These baits almost always sink, they have to. But, you can run them at almost any depth in the water column.

I like to have two styles of lipless crankbaits in my tackle box. One in a bait fish pattern like the Strike King Red Eye Shad. You can't go wrong with this bait. It can be extremely productive.

http://bit.ly/1SafnAw

I also like to have a craw pattern available. Both of these types of baits let you fish anywhere in the water column and switch from a bait fish to a crawfish depending on what the fish are biting that day. I like Xcalibur's Real Craw lipless crankbait with the matte finish. Any of these baits from bluish to darker reds seem to produce well.

http://bit.ly/1oXzg3e

Hard Swimbaits

I absolutely love to fish hard swimbaits. These come in many designs and are usually made of hard plastic with a jointed body. The joints are often metal hinges of different kinds, but could also be made of a strong fabric like Dyneema. These baits typically do not have any diving bill. They are slow sinkers and will have a tendency to slightly rise when retrieved. Many times they also include a couple of large rattles. The jointed body makes for a great realistic swimming action. These baits can be retrieved on a variety of techniques and also do well trolled.

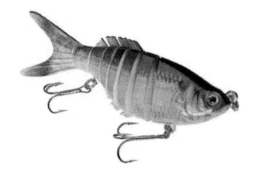

The Cabela's RealImage HDS hard swimbait combines an extremely realistic finish along with very life like swimming action.

http://bit.ly/2a1e0T6

The SPRO BBZ-1 Shad is a perfect example of this type of bait although I do usually prefer 2 treble hooks on baits like this.

http://bit.ly/1Q6PSvu

Jerk Baits

A seasoned favorite amongst bass anglers for suspended and colder water bass. These baits are longer minnow-shaped profiles, available in lots of different sizes and colors. With a slight twitch and stop type of retrieve, a stop and go, or even as a more slow and steady retrieve underwater, these baits can get finicky or cold bass to bite. This is often the default lure of choice in Winter and early Spring conditions. Another option is to use suspending jerk baits that typically dive deeper, jerking it, almost teasing and tempting the bass to come up and bite at it.

The Lucky Craft Pointer style of hard jerk bait is ideal. You can get it in a slightly smaller 78, or slightly larger 100 model.

http://bit.ly/1S6CRVc

Jigs

Some have described these trusted tackle as "lead head and hook with dressing." Their added features could take the shape of rubber or plastic skirts or soft plastic baits for bodies instead of skirts. Most bass experts combine them with a crawfish, or other plastic bait as a "trailer". Even strips of scented and colored pork skin can be added creating what is call a "jig and pig."

Chances are, if you're friends with a lot of fishermen, one of them will make his own jigs. In that case, you may prefer to use his hand made ones and have confidence in them. On the commercial side, jigs come in many styles and shapes with different functions. A swim jig will have a flatter head for planing in the water. A bottom jig may have a football shaped head for added movement when pulled over rocky bottoms. A flipping jig may have more of a bullet shaped head. The hook sizes, lengths, and skirt styles can vary also.

Strike King makes an excellent swim jig with nice shad patterns on the skirts. I like the little bit of red paint on the head and usually trim the fiber weed guard to even with the top of the hook point.

http://bit.ly/1NocfwU

I like the Chompers football head jig. The skirt is tough, the paint stays on the head, and I like the slight curve to the hook shank putting the point of the hook in more of a stand up position when fished on the bottom.

http://bit.ly/1N8rUFF

Punisher makes an excellent hair jig. I prefer this in brown or black. This is another great Winter time bait for fishing low and slow. Additionally, hair jigs are tough and don't get torn up like soft plastics do almost every cast. You can keep casting and catching without having to take the time to re-rig or fix a soft plastic you'd fish the same way. Lastly, if used as a crawfish imitation, the wire weed guards look a lot like antennae which I prefer over a fiber weed guard sometimes.

http://bit.ly/1N8sxit

Poppers

Poppers are top water lures that carry long-range punch. The retrieve with these kinds of lures are jerky or move in relatively one spot for a duration of time. They are called poppers because they are designed with a concave mouth or head opening that cups the water and pushes it forward upon each twitch of the retrieve. This creates a popping and disturbance of the water on the surface. They can be quite effective or on days with the right conditions that are early or late and flat calm waters. These baits can be in the shape of fish, frogs, fish, mice, cicadas, or other prey.

A top water strike is one of the most exciting things in fishing. It's often flat calm and near dead silent interrupted by an explosion of water and a big fish inhaling the bait from the surface. Sometimes the fish hit it so hard, their whole body leaves the water.

It's important not to react instantly and try to set the hook right away. With top water fishing, you want to see the strike, wait just a second to be sure the fish has it fully in its mouth, then set the hook. Often fish will hit this bait while you pause it between twitches.

The Skitter pop is an excellent top water popper with a bait fish design. It also includes a dressed rear treble hook.

http://bit.ly/1SzE4n5

The Rebel Crick Hopper is a small popper that can be good for all kinds of pan fish including bass. It looks very much like a grasshopper and is vigorously attacked in most freshwater locations.

http://bit.ly/1Q6RoxQ

Spinner baits

Spinner baits are artificial baits that are specifically designed for the purpose of tantalizing the fish. It is very similar to a jig, but with a blade that runs above the hook attached to a wire arm. It spins and can imitate a school of baitfish. It is meant to provoke, make a strike calling on the fish's natural instinct to feed and or defend. It optimizes your chances of securing strikes if you couple it with a trailer hook. Baits may have a single blade or many blades. They can vary in shape and function as well as color. Rotation, color, skirts, fluttering action all work together to simulate movement and prey on the move.

Having a spinner bait with some red in it, simulates blood or wounded prey to our underwater predator, triggering yet again their natural instincts and feeding response, increasing your odds of getting a bite.

http://bit.ly/1oXDDeH

Inline Spinner

An inline spinner is very descriptive of its design. Instead of the hook and spinner being separated by a length of bent wire, the wire is a straight shaft and the hook, usually a treble hook, is at the bottom of the shaft. Along the shaft is some kind of body to the bait. And the spinner blade is attached to the shaft with a clevis which allows it to fully spin when retrieved through water. This is an excellent panfish bait of all kinds. Even trout find it irresistible.

There are a variety of sizes and colors of inline spinners made by Mepp's. I prefer one about 1/8 oz, with a silver or gold blade and dressed hook.

http://bit.ly/1S6GRVF

Soft Plastics

Plastic Worms

There are a vast array of worms available on the market. For avid bass anglers they are a necessity. The technique to master is hooking them properly. When hooking a worm for bass fishing, it is of utmost importance to ensure that you thread it properly. Get a lot of the body onto the hook, and on straight. Otherwise, it may spin and mess up your presentation in the water. When we think of the soft plastic fishing worm, most of us probably think of the original Creme worm or a curly tail plastic worm. Those baits still exist and still work just fine. Today, we often think of baits like the Yamamoto senko or a Zoom Trick Worm.

Yamamoto Senko

http://bit.ly/1SajKM4

Zoom Trick Worm

http://bit.ly/1SajSex

Grubs

Grubs are a very common soft plastic bait. They usually have a rounded curly tail and come in all sizes. They can be used the same as plastic worms, but probably perform best when you swim them on the retrieve letting the tail wiggle the whole way back stimulating bites. Grubs can be extremely versatile. They can be used alone, fished weedless, on jigs, on worm hooks, used as a trailer on spinner baits and skirted jigs, or suspend it below a float.

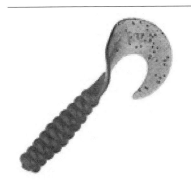

Berkley Power Grubs with Powerbait scent are an extremely effective soft plastic bait. Many times, I tie on a small pumpkinseed power grub with a 1/8 oz. jig head and troll it behind me to my first fishing location just to see how well the fish are biting that day. I would often pick up one or two fish immediately.

http://bit.ly/1SajYCY

I believe the Powerbait scent in these grubs adds tremendously to their effectiveness. Under the right circumstances, you could go a whole day using this bait and never change. That is particularly true for river smallmouth.

Crawfish

Crawfish are an excellent bass bait, especially for smallmouth. A three or four inch natural looking crawfish is deadly in a river environment. It is easy to bury an offset hook Texas rigged in a crawfish body with moving claws and legs. Even better, many jig heads with wire or fiber weed guards only adds to the profile looking like antennae or some other extremity.

My favorite soft plastic crawfish is the Zoom Speed Craw. I've had the most luck with this bait in this profile category. It isn't as realistic as other crawfish, but I think it has better swimming action with the claws if that's how you plan to retrieve it. A three inch speed craw in pumpkinseed or green pumpkin is ideal for river smallmouth fishing.

http://bit.ly/1Mu8YRH

My other favorite is the three inch Yum Craw Papi in natural crawdad or green pumpkin color. This one still swims with the claws, but not as well as the speed craw, but looks more realistic. The tail is solid, but the body is hollow and allows for a great place to insert the point of an offset hook while Texas rigging these baits for total weedlessness. You can easily set the hook on bites and the hook point will puncture through the top of the bait into the fish's mouth. These Yum baits are also scented which only adds to their effectiveness slowly fished on the bottom.

http://bit.ly/23uvQIw

Swimbaits

There are more soft plastic swimbaits than hard swimbaits on the market. The most effective seem to be some kind of paddle tail design, usually in a minnow profile. Of course, there have always been the old swim shad and sexy shad which are still effective too, but now we have a broader design choice in the market. I like a natural colored, white belly, silver sided, black or dark top minnow swimbait. You can rig them on a regular jig head for beset results or a keel weighted hook for more weedlessness.

Swimbait minnows cast out fast and far, allowing to let it fall and dangle, quiver down, with lots of slack, might prove just what the fish ordered.

The Bass Assassin Sea Shad might be my favorite soft plastic swimbait ever. It's one of the most productive baits I've ever used and I really enjoy using them. This is easily one of my top five all-time favorite baits. I feel more confident in the thinner minnow profile rather than thicker bodied shad profiles of other swimbaits. This bait just flat out produces fish. Here too, I have gone full days fishing this one bait and never changed lure types.

http://bit.ly/1S6KFpQ

Soft Jerk Bait

These can be used to great effect in the same manner as a regular jerk bait, but can be dropped to the bottom quite successfully as well to tease out our deep-water predator, swimming around for food and feast.

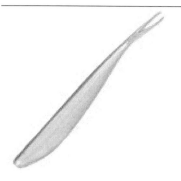

The Zoom Fluke or Super Fluke are excellent Fall and Spring time soft plastic jerk baits. They seem to do best in white or pearl.

http://bit.ly/1NogtEx

Tubes

Tube jigs and Power tubes that are scented, are other options. The soft, natural chewy substance, tricks the fish, into not wanting to let go and have another chew, thus increasing your odds of landing it safely. These baits can be versatile and resemble swimming bait fish, but more likely crawfish on the bottom. They can be rigged and fished a variety of ways.

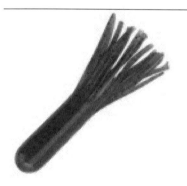

Berkley Power Bait tubes are an excellent scented choice for a tube pattern. They work great in pumpkinseed, dark brown, green pumpkin, and black with blue flake.

http://bit.ly/1Muajbd

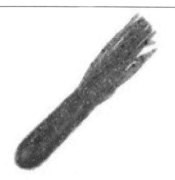

Coffee Tubes are one of the most scented baits you'll find. Something about a strong smell, even of something like coffee, can really trigger bites from fish like bass.

http://bit.ly/22ugBcB

Lizards

Lizards are soft plastic baits made by several companies, usually in the five or six inch range. They can be fished on jig heads, Texas rigged, weightless, skimmed on top water, Carolina rigged, and flipped into cover. These baits present more of a creature bait profile with swimming appendages and tails. Green pumpkin, black and blue flake, and purple are all good colors for lizard baits.

The six inch Zoom Lizard is a great bait to Texas or Carolina rig. You can fish it in and around weeds, on the bottom, or even swim it on top. Lizards tend to work best in green pumpkin, purple, and june bug colors.

http://bit.ly/1SMFmMa

Top Water

Surface, top water and or buzz baits: Acting almost like a spinner bait, but with a curved helicopter like blade that enables it to surface with speed and make a bubbly disturbance. This is a popular choice for many a bass enthusiasts. It attracts the attention of the bass, by creating a disturbance along the surface like a fleeing minnow or other prey, triggering their basic feeding instincts and hunter impulse to strike.

A buzz bait like the Booyah Pond Magic in white has the power to raise a fish or two from the depths.

http://bit.ly/1qHZ5WO

Top water baits with rattles are another all-time favorite, with slack in the line, walking the dog, makes for an enticing presentation for the fish below. However, the conditions must be right for this technique. A windy, choppy water day probably won't be good for a top water presentation.

There's nothing more well known for being able to present the walk the dog action than Heddon's Zara Spook.

http://bit.ly/1qoYuc5

Chatter Bait

A chatter bait is relatively new to the fishing scene as well. You can think of this lure as a combination of the wobble and disturbance of a crankbait, but the flashy blade of a spinner bait. The metal blade is shiny, but positioned up front vertically through a connection with a snap to the line. The effect is a rotational wobble in the water similar to the scrounger head's plastic cup or bill. This bait has the silicone skirt of a jig or spinner bait, but many fishermen also add a soft plastic trailer. I prefer a paddle tail soft plastic swimbait trailer. This can act as a great search bait to locate fish. You can show them a little more flash in the water if visibility is lacking. It can also be retrieved with other techniques such as trolling.

The Z Man Chatterbait in green pumpkin and black with a silver blade is my choice. You can choose a number of trailers from the two soft plastic legs that come with it, to a crawfish, to a swimbait. I often opt for the swimbait trailer.

http://bit.ly/1qRfw3p

Spoons

For spoons, there are two broad categories, namely trolling and casting spoons. Weedless lures mostly have hooks with nylon or metal weed-guards that prevent snagging and or non-weedless spoons are also commonly used. How to tell which one to use, most bass anglers look for shape, weight and speed. The best way to find your way around in any tackle shop or box, is to practice and get to know the behavior and or success in different conditions. Trying to get to know the optimum retrieval and success rates, maybe even logging it in a personal journal as you undertake your fishing journey.

Spoons act/move in a fishlike manner in the water, trolled behind boats they are typically very effective and can also be cast and retrieved. Plugs are made of various materials, designed specifically to float, dive below the surface or sink when reeling them back or in. They simulate surface disturbance and entice fish with propellers or plastic skirts that move and flutter in the water.

Blue Fox makes a variety of casting spoons in various colors that have proven successful over time.

http://bit.ly/1TRij7H

One of my favorite spoons, which is actually a trolling spoon, is the Krocodile. Although it performs just as well casting. This type of spoon has a little more erratic action in the water rather than just the spinning action of most casting spoons. Some days you can troll this behind your boat and catch five different species in five minutes. It's that appealing to a broad range of fish.

http://bit.ly/1SzOjrM

Lure Scents

Sometimes a scented bait makes all the difference in the world. Some baits above have scent impregnated in them, but if you want an effective way to add scent to your baits, something like the Bio Edge bait scents can be just the thing. I keep a couple of these in my PFD storage pockets at the ready all the time. I particularly like them on soft plastics. The wand has scented attractant that sticks on the bait longer than a liquid. I like these in crawfish and minnow scents.

http://bit.ly/1V1rdAE

The Bio Edge Minnow Scent Wand.

http://bit.ly/1oXLA3N

A large tackle bag can be handy for carrying and storage of large numbers of tackle boxes.

http://bit.ly/2bhPAJ3

LURE RIGGING

Jig head: This is one of the easiest rigs you can use. Select the appropriate size, shape, and weight jig head you want to use. Estimate the length of the hook shank and where it will exit out the back of the soft plastic lure. Slide the nose of the bait onto the hook point, bending the plastic to run up the shank and exit at your pre-determined position. Make sure the exit is in the middle of the bait or it could cause it to helicopter in the water, twisting your line, if off center.

Texas Rig: this is considered and named specifically for rigging with a soft plastic. Use a sliding weight, usually bullet shaped, and a hook sufficient for the size bait you have chosen. Sharpen the hook and stick the point of the hook directly into the worm head, bring it out the side about 1/8 - 3/16" below the entry, thread it again. Rotate the hook around so the point is facing the worm's body. Lay it over the side to see where it should enter in order to hang straight. Position the work straight onto the hook if it is hanging. NOTE: if the worm is twisted, your line and action will pay the price and it will be less effective.

Carolina rig: This can easily be described as simply a variation of the standard, so-called "Texas Rig" (see below), great for use with plastic worms or other soft baits like lizards. Most expert bass anglers suggest using a heavier weight like 1/4 -1/2 oz. or more. Slide the weight onto the line, follow with three plastic beads, a barrel swivel, and a leader line (somewhat smaller than the main line).What this allows the bass angler to do is to get the bait to drop down to the bottom with speed and is especially recommended for fishing deep waters. The movement of the leader allows the bait to swim or move and rise above the bottom and fall slowly down. For most beginners this is easy to do and practice and is very versatile to get your routine rigging and tackle skills to improve. It's also a better way to avoid snags with the weight moved farther away from the hook. You won't be pulling the heavy bait directly into things like down wood as easily.

Nose rig: You can often take a small hook, a circle hook for example, and hook it through the nose of a soft plastic jerk bait. You can do this vertically, but horizontally works very well for weedlessness. Just remember to only reel, don't set it, after the fish hits it and you may want to give it an extra second or two since the hook is now further up at the head of the bait in case of a short strike.

Go Here to View a Video of Freshwater Lures to Keep in Your Freshwater Arsenal

https://youtu.be/P-XyTeD3RKY

Go Here to View My Three Favorite River Fishing Lure Types

https://youtu.be/NuIKDyA2DEU

TECHNIQUES AND RETRIEVES

Technique Specific Rods and Staging of Rods

The true secret lies in what some call the one-two punch, teasing and enticing with a teaser lure and then following it up with a plastic worm, for example, on a second rod, for optimizing strikes and tipping the scales in your favor. Now we are getting into the mastery portion of the skills involved in fishing. In chess, a good player will think 3, 4, 5 moves ahead. You can do the same when you start to master your skills fishing. The whole purpose of having multiple rods on a boat is not simply just to have them, but to have technique or lure specific rods rigged and ready to go at a moment's notice. So you quietly pull up to your usual fishing spots where you know fish like to hold. You can start with a cast to it with a spinner bait. If no hits, follow it up immediately with a crankbait. If not hits still, follow it up with a swimbait. And finally a worm or crawfish soft plastic. If you're reasonably certain fish are there, and you haven't scared them off, these types of successive presentations can help you pattern the fish for the day. The pattern being the lure size, type, color, and retrieve. It may take some persistence to determine this too. It may take as many as 5, 10, or 20 casts, maybe with the same lure before the fish strikes. If you're reasonably certain the fish are still there, don't give up.

Some days you'll notice that it is the green pumpkin grub that's the ticket. Some days you'll notice that it's the 6" purple lizard they prefer. Some days, in the morning, they prefer the pumpkinseed tube, but that bite dies down and in the afternoon and evening, they start hitting natural colored swimbaits.

You can do a similar technique as above with your rod staging, but with the same lure and rod. Let's say you have on a 4" minnow soft plastic swimbait. You can cast it out and retrieve it quickly burning it back close to the surface. If no hits, you can try again, but this time with a slower, but middle of the water column steady retrieve. If no hits, you can try slow rolling it back periodically bumping the bottom with it. If still nothing, you can try retrieving it with pauses or twitches. You can yo-yo it up and down jigging it vertically and horizontally in the water column. Lastly, you could cast it out and just dead stick it on the bottom. All different presentations you can try with the same bait.

In fact, from an organization standpoint, if you're not moving too quickly with the wind or current, it might be good to try some or all of these techniques with the same rod and lure before moving onto your other rods and lures. That way, you can really narrow down what the fish are after that particular time and day not only regarding the particular bait, but how they want it presented.

Styles And Specialty Bass Fishing Techniques

Skipping

This technique might remind you a lot of throwing rocks onto the surface of the water to see it skip.

Spinning rods and reel combo is best used for this technique, perfect for fishing and reaching bass where they swim and hide under piers, docks and pontoons. Also useful for getting under and into underbrush and growth. Remember their comfort zone. On sunny days, bass look for shade, food and shelter and often rest here in shady areas, under cover of structure. To employ, simply boat up to a dock or other structure quietly, make a side arm cast at a low angle to the water with something like a soft plastic so it skips a couple of times to get up under the structure. Let the bait fall weightless. Chances are you'll get a hit right then. If not, you can employ a few twitches, jerks, or some other type of retrieve and try again.

Ripping

Some call this popping and dropping A medium power, fast action rod or better will likely be what is needed here. It might actually trick our bass friend into thinking there is a wounded prey around. Let the worm drop and settle to the bottom, remaining there for a period of time. Reel some slack out of the line, picking up the worm with a long, sharp upsweep of the rod tip. Let her rip! Let it drop down again to the bottom, under tension while slowly lowering the rod tip. Keep on imitating live prey like this, moving, swimming, and bobbing about and your predator will strike it with a vengeance.

Drifting

Trailing behind the boat, covering the bottom, worms, crawfish, and creature soft plastic baits crawl and move, simulating prey in its purest form. Raise and lower it occasionally, looking natural and alluring to any bass in the vicinity hunting for a tasty morsel. This is a great technique on most fishing trips. I will often tie on a large Texas rigged worm as weedless as possible with no weight or only 1/16 and let it drift behind the boat while I move with the current and actively cast to targets out front. It will periodically grab onto structure on the bottom and then pop off suddenly going back to crawling its way along the bottom. It's a form of more passive fishing. But, the fish will eat it up. I often use a larger bait so as to have a chance at a larger fish while I may be making more finesse presentations actively up front. Some days, you don't have to cast or retrieve much at all. Just put in and float down all day drifting tubes or worms or craws and reel smallmouth in one after another.

Trolling

Another technique that can be brutal (for the fish) is trolling. At first I didn't like trolling because I'd always been on charter boats as a kid trolling for stripers in the bay. There's little activity on your part as the customer, you just reel them in like wet newspapers when the bait gets bit. You can get slow speeds and perfect the right pace to entice fish to action. You can instantly change speed and direction making some lures on opposite sides of your rigging slow down or speed up triggering more bites. You can troll any bait you want from a boat. Sometimes even idling speed or a trolling motor on the lowest setting may be too fast for some species in a power boat though. You can control the depth of crankbaits better by how fast you go. If you can rig up your boat so that the trolling rods are in front of you, you won't have to continually look back to check on them. This makes the act of trolling much more active and enjoyable. Then, when the action heats up and you get double or triple bites at the same time, it's really a heart pounding adventure.

There is a lake where my most successful fish catching technique has been trolling and it's been by a wide margin too over all other methods.

Drop-Shotting For Picky, Overfished Bass

There is a fairly new technique when it comes to bass fishing but it works great especially when bass are under a lot of pressure, it's called drop shotting. When you see other fishermen using worms and fishing the edges of creek channels, try this and fish the bottom of the channels instead of the edges. It's also good around boat docks and bridges and in shallow water when the bass are bedding.

When fishing the bottom of a channel try a small worm hook with a 3/16 ounce sinker or whatever weight you need to get down and stay there. If you have one already a bell sinker works great, but there are specific drop shot weights now.

Here is what you need to rig a drop shot:

A small octopus worm hook and an 1/8 to 1/2 ounce bell sinker or special drop shot sinker. Tie the hook on your line using a palomar knot and leave enough line after the knot for the depth you want the sinker below it. You're trying to get the lure the right length up the line to be in front of the fish while you can feel the sinker on the bottom. Tie the bell weight at the bottom of the line. It's that easy. Don't drag the bait or hop it, shake it, jiggle it in place. This action gives the lure an erratic tail wiggling action that can entice bass to bite. If your lake has a lot of fishing pressure from being fished so hard or the fish are just picky try this technique and see the results.

Walking the Dog

This is an angling technique that usually requires some time to master, but beginners should not shy away from trying it, for it is quite effective with bass. Casting over a relatively long distance, allow the bait to sit for a brief period of time, take up the slack, and with your rod tip pointed at the water, 90 degrees to the direction of your line, give it a jerk and immediately give the line a little bit of slack, then immediately move it backward and reel in any slack, then jerk again, and repeat all the way back. More or less a darting from side-to-side is made by the lure. You are in effect simulating the prey's elusive movements, enticing the hunter to follow, stalk, and hit. This might be your ace up your sleeve for hooking up fish on a good top water day.

Bobber Rigs and Slip Sinkers

Slip-bobbers, rigged with a 1/16 ounce jig, live bait like minnow, night-crawler or leech at its tip and, of course, all on a sharpened hooks can be extremely effective for all sorts of panfish. This is a great beginner technique and for kids.

Jiggling, lightly shaking, presenting this close to any emerging weeds or brush, underwater logs, trees, stumps, or cover, may prove successful.

Floating jig heads, with slip-sinker rig, with 2-3 foot leader have proven to be useful too, especially when kept close to the bottom, watching not to get snagged in the process. Weedless hooks can help you retrieve live bait and or that hooked fish, through very thick undercover.

Free Lining

Fishing in shallow waters may yield many a bass angler quite the haul. Casting a plain J hook with live bait and feed the line to the bait, allowing it to swim while slightly struggling on the hook will attract some certain attention. You can do this with no float, no weight, and either bail open or closed.

Experts would recommend if you are in the weeds or heavy slop, cover, and jungles underwater, to go heavier is the key. 20 lb. line the minimum and heavy power, fast action, sturdy bait-casting rod and reel combos to provide you with leverage to reel in your fish. A large struggling bluegill on the end of a line could yield you a monster size largemouth bass.

Flipping and Pitching

Flipping and pitching are two similar techniques often confused or used interchangeably. Both are usually performed with bait casting reels and heavier powered rods with faster actions in or around structure and cover.

Flipping is a short distance "cast" to a nearby object that may hold fish. The line, just above the reel is pulled away from the rod brining the lure up to the rod tip. The angler proceeds to swing the lure outward toward the object and releases the line back to the rod and reel allowing the lure to drop in on the object. This is usually performed with a jig type bait with a trailer, but could also be used with a worm. Anything that is a dead stick type bait presentation or it may include a few shakes and wiggles if the bait isn't hit immediately. A rapid succession of short flips can be placed in a short amount of time along a structured area that may hold fish. In this technique, the reel is never engaged.

Pitching is slightly different. It can be used with other baits for more moving and retrieving presentations. Often it is used to pitch a heavy weighted lure (like a jig) up high to punch down through grass mats. But, that isn't the only option. In this technique, the angler swings the lure back up into his non-rod hand. He lets go of the lure while downwardly sweeping his rod tip to "pitch" the lure out to a desired target while thumbing the reel spool. Think of it as sort of an underhand cast. The reel may be set to near free spool with this technique and all the control is done by the angler's thumb on the line. Upon contact, he can let the bait sit or begin his desired retrieve. Some reel models today have controls built in for pitching allowing the angler to press down on the release lever, pitch the bait, keeping the lever depressed while also thumbing the spool. As soon as he lets off the lever, the reel engages closed again. He doesn't need to engage a turn of the reel in order to lock the reel. Both of these techniques can be a quitter or softer way to get your bait in the water rather than a long and high cast where the lure creates a large splash upon entry. These types of settings and this technique can also be a way to make a quick succession of short casts to potentially awaiting fish. More casts and more bait time in the water equals greater chances of hooking up.

Night and Winter Fishing

Dropping the lure or bait right in front of the fish while not having them expend a lot of energy is the key for these times and conditions. Water tends to be cooler and all your approaches, strategies, and techniques need to slow down a notch. Bass also tend to school, during these times. Knowing this fact can help you in acquiring your target better and increasing your odds of getting a hit under these unusual or specialty conditions.

Again, understanding what bass actually eat, where and when, will help you with choosing and presenting the most effective, appropriate and tempting bait (whether live or artificial). Drawing on the natural diet of the fish, can assist you in improving your baits and lures appearance, strategy, tactics, and eventual success. Bass, as a predator will be looking for certain shapes, colors and familiar movement. Plastic worms and crawfish are popular choices, but are usually sized down in Winter. Another good lure option in these times is the hair jig. Either a dark brown or black hair on a small 1/8 ounce or less jig head. You can fish this bait the same as you would a small tube, worm, or crawfish, only slower.

Fly Fishing for Bass

For fly fishing for bass can provide some of the most exciting fishing there is. Smallmouth bass are also excellent for fly fishing, but they prefer slightly cooler waters and are not as ever present as the largemouth variety.

The behavior of the largemouth bass is also influenced considerably by the top temperature of the water. On hot summer days, they usually feed during the early morning hours and then again during the last few hours of daylight, when the sun isn't as bright and the water temperature is cooler. Bass are generally found in areas of the water that have a lot of vegetation and cover. They spend a lot of time near the water's edge among the grasses, reeds, and other plants.

Many fly fishermen fishing for largemouth bass use bass bugs and poppers in these areas. Poppers were designed as a surface lure to be skipped across the top of the water in a series of quick retrieves. Other good fly patterns for largemouth bass or the Muddler Minnow and the Wooly Worm. There are some fly fishermen that prefer to use streamers and bucktails.

Fly rods and line weights are typically written as Xwt where the x is a number. For example, you can have 8wt, 9wt, etc. All rods are matched to fly lines according to weight. So if you have an 8wt rod, you'll need an 8wt fly line although you can safely go one number above or below the weight if need be.

It is important to use the correct fly line with the appropriate rod weight or it will significantly affect your casting performance.

Some rods are multi-rated (7-8wt, 7-8-9wt, etc.). The advantage to a rod like this is that you have a variety of fly lines that you can use with the same rod. The disadvantage is that you will be sacrificing flexibility in the rod itself.

Selecting a fly rod depends a lot on what type of fish you will want to catch. Some rods are better suited for smaller fish and bigger fish. Here is an idea of the weight of rod you will need for certain situations:

4-6 Weight: Pan fish and small bass, 4wt is for delicate presentation, 5wt is good for smallmouth on creeks or smaller rivers, 6wt is best on bigger waters or in windy conditions.

7-8 Weight: Give extra power to land smallmouth bass and bigger largemouths in rivers or reservoirs; work best with bigger flies with more wind resistance.

When fly fishing for bass the fly is worked differently than it is for trout. Poppers are worked not only for their appearance but also for their sound. Generally, when a fly is cast for bass it should be allowed to remain unmoving for a longer period of time then for trout. It is estimated that 60% of bass strikes are made on a still fly. Bass tend to inspect your fly for some time before making the decision whether to take it or not. It is important to remember while fly fishing, that the warmer the water, the longer it may take the bass to take a fly.

At times fly fishermen like to tease the bass with repeated casts over the area where they think he's holding. Teasing can sometimes be a very effective method in bringing a lazy fish up for a strike when nothing else seems to work. Fly fishing for largemouth bass can be a wonderful, exciting experience.

You can find an excellent selection of bass flies at Orvis.

http://bit.ly/2bIOWoU

More Recent and Advanced Fishing Techniques

Large Swimbaits

I love swimbait fishing. And most of what I do is with three to six inch lures that are usually soft plastic, but also some hard jointed baits too. It seems there's two distinct categories of swimbait fishing.

Those of us probably like me and you making up the majority of the fishing population who use moderately priced baits that are about the same size as other soft plastics in our tacklebox.

Then there is a class of fisherman who has taken it to the ultimate extreme. They primarily prefer to use large swimbaits, some plastic, some hard, that might be up to 12 inches long. You may have seen large and very realistic looking rainbow trout soft plastic swimbaits. Or a largemouth bass realistic single jointed hard bait called a glide bait.

The difference here is size and cost. Many of us use large baits from time to time so this is mostly a cost differential. The large tackle manufacturers are producing lures that can be sold for the most quantity at the right market price the majority of the market will pay. The large swimbaits may be commercially produced or home made artistic works. You may see them in marketplaces like ebay for upwards of $900 per bait.

It's really a preferred technique or a lifestyle thing at that point. Definitely a subset of angler who is willing to invest that much in one lure to catch a huge bass.

And it does work. Of course, you have to have a population of huge bass to catch which is why I think this technique is often seen out west in California. A warm climate and a body of water where bass may have been fed stocked trout before could result in a very large catch.

SPRO has entered this market sort of bridging the gap between these two group by producing designer, Bill Siematel's rat swimbait/wakebait that can range from six to ten inches in length, but not cost over $30 or so. You may also see similar baits from other companies in the form of large bull shad.

The SPRO Rat swimbait is extremely popular.

http://bit.ly/2bzJYH2

The Deps Slide Swimmer glide bait.

http://bit.ly/2c8LEZR

Alabama Rig

The Alabama rig absolutely took tournament fishing by storm a couple of years ago. Some even questioning to allow its use at all or not. In essence, the Alabama rig attempts to mimic a swimming school of bait fish. If you've ever trolled for striped bass in some place like the Chesapeake bay, you're probably familiar with the umbrella rig. The Alabama rig is simply a castable umbrella rig. It is usually rigged with four or five inch swimbaits on jig heads on a wire frame attached to a single head with a hook eye. Needless to say, this bait can get heavy real fast necessitating the need for a heavy duty swimbait rod.

The various arms of the umbrella rig can be terminated in a swimbait on a jig head, or teaser baits only with a trailing hooked bait, or other teasers like spinner blades only.

Now several manufacturers make them and you can even mold your own. The rigs can be difficult to store in transport in normal tackle storage options. However, it produces big fish after schools of bait.

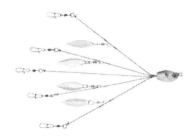

YUM makes an Alabama rig called the Yumbrella.

http://bit.ly/2c8HZeC

Ned Rig

The Z-man Ned rig is a simple variation, but often talked about as if it's an entirely different technique. Quite simply, it's a small senko type worm with a mushroom shaped jig head. Who would have ever thought of putting a jig head in a soft plastic, right? Well, it's taken on its own identity and proven to be a very effective finesse fishing technique.

One of the points of differentiation concerning Z-man's products is the Elaztech plastic used. This material is very soft, but super tough at the same time increasing the life of each bait. Be careful when coming into contact with other plastics as they may chemically melt one another.

This bait and technique was specifically designed by and for the mid-west fisherman. Give the Ned rig a shot when all other techniques are failing to produce. You can now also find the Ned rig Shroomz jig heads compatible with a list of other small plastic bait profiles like hula stick, jerkbaits, and tubes.

The Ned rig's finesse TRD worm, with its dimpled texture meant to be paired with the Z-man Shroomz jig heads.

http://bit.ly/2bzByPO

Whopper Plopper

I remember watching videos of Larry Dahlberg producing whopper ploppers by hand in his workshop a few years ago on the hunt for muskies. But, lately, they have become commercially available in a couple different sizes for largemouth bass made by River2sea.

It's a different take on top water fishing. It isn't the typical popper. It's also not a buzzbait or propeller bait. It's sort of a combination. The wire extends through the bait attached to a tail section with a spinning and rotating hard tail. The water passing over the tail section makes it spin and on each revolution it makes a plopping sound on the surface of the water.
You can get the whopper plopper in two sizes from three and a half to five inches.

Larry Dahlberg's Whopper Plopper from River2sea.

http://bit.ly/2coQaHP

Spy Baiting

Spy baiting is another finesse technique refined in recent years that comes to us from Japan of all places. The lure resembles a thin profiled minnow hard body, as you would expect with any jerkbait or crankbait, but it has a propeller with tuned blades on each end at the nose and tail.

It's referred to as the "technique of silent capture." Anglers were producing these lures on their own, but several companies have since picked up the design for commercial distribution.

It is fished on very light spinning gear with a very slow to moderate retrieve. The steady retrieve imparts the action into the lure. And it is very subtle. It is not a violent wide wobble like with a billed bait. It will list or "roll" gently from side to side in a swimming action causing the bait to flash it's sides as you see with bait fish in the water. If you pause on the retrieve, it will slowly sink with a shimmying action until you retrieve again.

There's more than one way this bait and technique entice fish to bite when they are otherwise finicky. Consider this technique when stealth, no sound, and slow speed are required.

Lucky Craft makes an American version of a prop spy bait.

http://bit.ly/2bGuLWq

DIY LURES

You may get tired of purchasing packages of soft plastics over and over again. Or you may be interested in a new challenge or skill. In which case, producing your own lures, may be in the cards for you. This can be a developed skill and quite messy at times. But, a little practice can have you pumping out bulk loads of your own soft plastics you use often. You can color them exactly to how you like them or even add in your own scents and salt. You can find molds in common bass bait patterns like senkos, brush hogs, river bugs, grubs, trick worms, flukes (soft jerkbait), and swimbaits.

A bass fisherman pouring and making his own soft plastic lures is the equivalent of a trout fisherman tying his own flies. It adds another layer of challenge, and therefore, reward when you actually haul in a fish on your own creation with your own time and effort.

The Do It Soft Plastics Molds.

http://bit.ly/2bOTYxJ

Injection molding into milled aluminum molds is one of the best ways to get reliable pours and high quality mold outputs almost every time. Many molds have multiple cavities allowing you to produce up to four lures at a time.

Once you have the molds and injectors paid for, you can quickly see the cost savings in plastisol. It's estimated that a gallon of plastisol could produce 400 lures for around $50. Imagine trying to buy 400 name brand lures even in packages of 10.

You can buy your own plastisol and make soft plastics in bulk.

http://bit.ly/2bCSb2e

It's as simple as melting the plastisol in the microwave and injecting into the molds. Be sure you have a work surface you can get a little dirty. You can even reuse all of your old soft plastics for re-molding. The plastic sets up quickly in the mold and lures are ready to fish within minutes of pouring.

Note: Be extremely careful with hot plastic. It can severely burn your skin and sticks so it is very hard to get off in a hurry. A pair of insulated gloves might not be a bad idea when handling the hot plastic or tools.

PUTTING IT ALL TOGETHER

Keep a Journal

Once you have successfully put all the pieces together, it is important to be able to replicate it in the future. Or to at least know what is most likely to work again. This will contribute to helping you "learn" the water. Keeping a simple journal of all of the relevant information or conditions and time of year can go a long way to being successful again that same time next year. You can always refer back to what worked and what didn't in the past.

A pad and paper, spiral or composition notebook can work just fine if you prefer to keep hard copies. However, these can get lost or destroyed and you can't search through them easily. For me, my blog serves somewhat as my journal. It's easy to search through and help others find information as well. Everything is dated and I include all the relevant conditions that contributed to my success that day or time of year.

A combination of some electronic platform like that, float plans, video with time stamps, and GPS info can all paint a clearer picture to compile a fishing journal for you.

A Plan of Action

Most times during the Summer when I would guide clients on a half or full day fishing trip, I had a plan of action for the day. I had some idea of what the conditions were and what the fishs' behavior was like because I was likely fishing the day or night before. One location, in particular, I liked to take people on the river allowed us a variety of opportunities for various fishing styles, techniques, and to score multiple species on the same trip. Here's what it looked like. A map of this location is highlighted below.

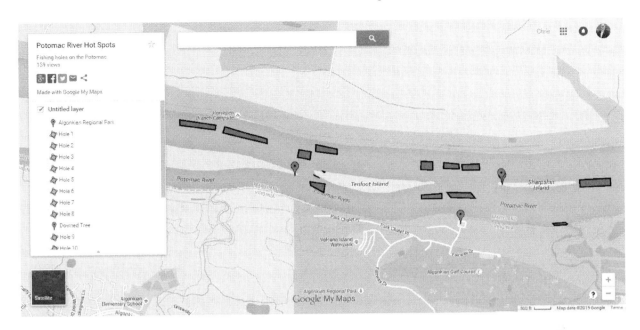

After my introduction at the ramp, we'd launch and could start fishing right away. There is usually some grass, rocks, and holes right at the launch. Many times, we could catch smallmouth immediately. That's a good way to start a trip and lets you know they are actually biting that day. I'd start small with a small Berkley Power Grub on a 1/8 oz. jig head or a small tube bait. Clients could cast and "swim" the grub back, twitch it, or fish the bottom low and slow with the tube. I had all of this rigged ahead of time.

After we had fished those structures pretty hard, we'd move on. We'd make a few casts on the downstream side of an island and work the bank and the eddy. We didn't spend too much time here.

Then, there was a couple of long deeper holes, we would go up above and drift tubes and senkos as we went with the current down the length of the hole. This usually produced several fish and we could drift this area three or four times back to back. There was also a large sunken tree trunk and a rock pile at the head of one of the holes that held fish we picked up as we went over it. This was slow, silent fishing on the bottom. We would most likely use no weight or as little as possible to only lightly bump the bottom or pull through any grass. If the grass was in full bloom, we'd fish the grass line and open areas in the grass mats hard with soft plastics of all kinds.

After we'd exhausted that area, it was time to move up stream. We'd cast out our three or four inch minnow swimbaits and troll them upstream as we gently go to our destination. The same grub trolled worked well here too. A couple of fish could usually be landed this way in a 10 or 15 min. tirp up to the top of the same island. This is a great way to make use of time. Why just move with no bait in the water? That's a 0% chance of catching anything. At least this way, we had to get somewhere and had the possibility of catching fish too. Often we did.

Toward the top of this island, there was a sandy bank with a steep drop off with over hanging trees and brush. This is where the largemouth would hold. We'd cast up on the bank or a foot within it and slowly pull soft plastics off it into the mouth of a waiting largemouth. A few fish could be picked up here as well, often on successive casts. Although, fast and furious action, initially, being largemouth, they wised up and got tired of this more quickly than the smallmouth. We made a few casts, caught a few fish, and moved on. At the upstream tip of the island was a large eddy and slack water formed by where the current came diagonally between the two islands. This eddy line held fish and the shallow slack water inside it did too. There were small smallmouth and large numbers of large bluegill/sunfish. The grub worked well at catching them both.

There was also a large pool formed at the top of the island in higher water. Downed wood held fish there some times. We could rest in here and hold position out of the wind and current. It also allowed us to park our boats on the bank and fish the eddy from shore. While out of our boats, we'd cross to the other side of the island and fish a short section of bank that had another downed tree trunk and small eddy. Largemouths and rock bass held just off this bank.

Out away from the island, on the other side of the line the eddy made, was a deeper hole created by the current. This hole was also good to drift soft plastics through several times. We could position our boats facing upstream, cast out two different soft plastics, like a senko and a tube or a crawfish, and place our rods up front in outward pointing rod holders like outriggers. The current would gently take us backwards dragging our baits along. We can watch our rod tips for the first sign of a bite. At the same time as those two baits in the water, we could cast out laterally into the deeper water with crankbaits, swimbaits, and jigs. This was an opportunity to get multiple hook ups. Not just between us, but within your own rod system. You may be fighting one fish and another picks up your soft plastic on the bottom and he's hooked. This is an exciting and potentially chaotic scenario, but fun for a guiding client. It's hard not to get tangled in this scenario, but we managed and had a great time doing it.

Up next would be paddling up to the third island in this chain of three in the river. Towards the downstream tip of that island, there was a large tree trunk, half sunken that never moved even in high water. This area held rock bass. We'd change our baits to the Power grub again or a three inch Zoom Speed Craw. If we cast to the end of the trunk under water, we could catch smallmouth and rock bass here. When they stopped biting there, we would cross over between the islands. There was a deep pool and often an open area in some grass we would fish on the opposite side between the islands. It was easy to sit on the grass mats and cast to the edges of other grass lines or into the open areas and score many smallmouth.

Next it was time to go for the big boys. There were two long deep holes, sort of a broken channel on the opposite side of the river. The water here could get up to eight to 10 feet deep. This offered an opportunity for many drifts with large soft plastics. Or if the current wasn't flowing much or if wind was in an opposing direction, we'd sit and spot fish. But, mostly this was a long drift with two or three large soft plastics unweighted or with a 1/16 oz. bullet weight lightly bumping the bottom with the current. We went big here. Especially in late Summer, Early Fall. A large six or seven inch Texas rigged senko, sometimes scented, was the ticket. We picked up many 18 inchers out of this area.

We could also fish the deeper water with crankbaits and this is where I'd change gears some after we wore out the big fish. I'd break out my fly rod and give it to one of the clients. This is about the time the sun would start to get lower and the wind would die down allowing for better fly casting ability.

We could hang in this deeper water area or go over to the far bank and fly cast for some of the smaller smallmouth in the shallows. This allowed clients to get in two distinctly different types of fishing in one trip. They'd have fun catching the small guys in numbers on the fly.

As the sun was going down, this allowed us to do a long, leisurely float back down the opposite bank, fishing the channel, and catching fish the whole way back to the end of the island. There we'd fish the opposite side of the river we launched from and hit two deeper holes for a few last fish before heading directly back across to the ramp from where we launched.

We could accomplish all of the above in a half day, four hour trip on the river putting in and taking out from one location.

CATCH AND RELEASE FISHING

The catch and release method was first introduced in the 1950s. It was designed to reduce the rising costs of restocking hatchery raised fish and was normally used for fish not meant for consumption. Popular consensus today does not consider bass as a food fish, and thus this technique is widely used in Florida bass fishing.

In general, it can be good over time to remove a few smaller fish from the breeding population to better manage the fishery. Fisheries scientists actively manage this kind of thing all the time at various bodies of water in a given area. You don't want to remove the monsters in a breeding class from a fishery.

Doing your part to protect nature and conserve it for future generations, is mandatory and regulated. Using barb-less hooks and or removing them if required. Holding the fish in the water as much as possible, gently unhooking, minimizing the trauma and damage to the fish, especially the jaw, is crucial. Support the fish and let it go with the current, swimming away and left to live another day, for many battles more to come!

Do all you can to understand and adhere to licensing, permits, closed season stipulations, minimum size and catch limits. These and other measures are there to protect and to minimize the risk of over-fishing and species becoming extinct. Now, catch and release fishing all the time, by itself, is not a good thing. If you come upon a fisheries management situation where you are asked or allowed to harvest certain species, sizes, or numbers, then by all means, take advantage and maybe feed your family that night too.

There was a reservoir I used to fish where white perch would over populate and they asked anglers to harvest them without limit. I periodically took advantage and made some small perch fillets, even fish tacos that were great. I'd even save one small little perch for the cat. Cooked pan fried then chopped it up like cat food. He loved it!

If the environment presents itself to where you can take advantage of the natural resources, and you're well within the legal limits, there's nothing wrong with partaking once in a while.

FISHING ETHICS

The way you are perceived and accepted by fellow anglers may not be high on your list of priorities when learning how to fish. However, there are some common courtesy points that all fishermen should abide by to make the experience as pleasant as possible for everyone.

While the rules of politeness may not always be accented in our society as much as it once was, we should have respect for our fellow sportsmen just as they should have the same respect for you.

This also extends beyond treating others with respect, it also entails respecting the resources on which you are fishing. The water, the banks, the woods, and all of outdoors should be treated with common courtesy so it is not damaged for future generations or current property owners. To leave no mark where you have passed in your fishing adventure is showing the ultimate respect.

Here are a few common suggestions of courtesy you should follow when fishing:

1. Wait your turn at a boat ramp. Don't jump in front of others with larger boats to launch. There may be no established right of way at the ramp. Be sure to follow the rules on all signage at the ramp in which you are launching. Generally, I like the elevator principle. People must get out first in order for you to get in. Outside of that, courtesy goes a long way. If you're confused at all, just communicate with the other sportsmen around you to "direct traffic."

2. A section of water belongs to the first person fishing it. It is inconsiderate to crowd an angler who was there first.

3. Obey who has the right of way. Always be on the lookout in your surroundings. Don't assume that they see you. Don't encroach on other stopped or drifting power boats while they are fishing.

4. A slow moving or stationary angler has the right to remain where he/she is. If you are moving, avoid the water they are fishing and quietly move around the angler in position in the water.

5. If an angler is resting the water, or allowing the water to calm down after some form of disturbance, let them be. Generally, after a fish has been caught, the act of the fight scares the rest of the fish and makes them

hesitant to bite again, so they rest the water until it is fishable again. They might be planning their next move too. When an angler is resting the water, it is his or her water. Don't jump in without permission.

6. A person working upstream generally has the right of way over someone fishing downstream.

7. Always yield to an angler with a fish on the line.

8. Do not enter the water directly in front of someone already in the water.

9. Do not litter. If you brought it in, take it out. Better yet, always try to leave the water or area you are fishing with more than you came in with. Leave the area cleaner than you found it.

10. Try not to make tracks whenever possible.

11. Wave or wave back to other boaters on the water. It is a friendly thing to do and shows that we are all happy to be out there. It also acknowledges that you see them and they see you.

12. Obey all state and local fishing laws and rules.

13. Never attempt to land someone's fish for them if they have not asked you to help. You do not want the responsibility of losing some guy's lifetime fish.

14. Do not dictate what kind of lure to use unless asked. It is downright amazing what fish will hit on. Let your buddies pattern the fish themselves. If you have good luck and a fellow angler isn't, you might say, "This green pumpkin grub really seems to be working, I have an extra if you would like to try it."

15. Respect others' property rights. That means fences and gates. Close all gates behind you. No trespassing means NO trespassing. You can find out who owns the property and ask permission. Many folks will happily say yes. And you can offer to go above and beyond by cleaning up trash or mowing some of the property another time, etc. However, no really means NO. Sometimes, the landowner may even own a particular stretch of river bed bottom. This is rare, but it is a real thing.

16. Just in case you end up in a situation where some ignorant person violates any of the suggestions above, explain as politely as possible their error. It sometimes works. Maybe no one ever told them about angling etiquette or

boating rules or laws.

17. If the person decides his or her fishing is more important than yours, do not stoop to their level. Move on. You probably won't catch anything with them there, and the stress of having to be around such people isn't worth it.

While fishing, your most likely confrontations will be with jet skiers and rowers in many locations, usually high school teams rowing crew who are out practicing. Jet skiers are out to have fun (rightly so) and rarely have been exposed to the same kind of etiquette that we anglers have. Nor have they been educated on the rules of the water. High school rowing teams often occupy some of the same boat ramps and practice on the same waters we fish. To us, it can often appear as though they think they own the place. A million kids running around, entitled coaches, a jammed up boat ramp that takes you 30 minutes to get out of because they are blocking the whole thing. That's ok. You can still use the principles above to navigate your way through these encounters.

Anticipate some of these and don't let anyone ruin your day on the water. Just going with it is better than killing yourself inside or, worse, a violent confrontation. We're all just here to do what we love and it just so happens there is not very much water (even less access points), and a lot of people. But, you have the advantage. You can launch and go where they cannot. If you routinely run into these problems, just consider looking up a different spot. There are many apps and online maps where you can plan your put in, take out, and fishing spots where you hopefully won't be bothered by these confrontations. Better yet, see if you know of someone who has property that might offer a good fishing location or launch site and get permission. Always ask, every time!

People fish to relieve stress, not create it. When you have someone trying to intrude on your peacefulness, it's best just to walk away rather than exacerbate it. Remember that a little common sense goes a very long way when it comes to basic etiquette.

This might not be the finest book on bass fishing ever written, but may the passion and contents inspire you to greatness as an avid and successful angler. If we can ignite confidence and excitement for fishermen and women, young and old, then these pages have succeeded.

May the fish come up to meet you. May your journey and journal grow, each entry teaching more, increasing confidence and aptitude!

May the pleasures of fishing and the many ways we can choose to actively to partake of it, bring you continued enjoyment, reward, and pleasure!

It is almost an impossibility to provide here for every unique condition and technique possible and we barely scratched the surface on most of the contexts bass anglers might find themselves.

As we have discovered throughout these pages, there is a lot more to fishing than meets the eye. Once you are familiar with the species, different bodies of water, sophisticated fishing equipment, accessories, familiarizing yourself with habits, patterns, nature, behavior, natural diet, preferred foods, mastering some basic skills, preparation, presentation, tackle, bait, lures, casting accuracy, knots, hooks and the intricacies and complexities in retrieval and landing, the journey has, but just begun. There is so much more to explore and learn about through the activity and sport, itself that we can almost say no more than, the water is calling, let's go!

We look forward to sharing more tips, strategies, and techniques with you and learning from each other.

RESOURCES AND OTHER BOOKS ON BASS FISHING

Retailers:

Rapala - **Save 10% on all orders at Rapala.com! Just enter code FISH10 at checkout.** http://bit.ly/1Vm01wg

Bass Pro Shops - http://bit.ly/1SaouRY

Cabela's Web Only Specials - http://bit.ly/2bzTOMr

Tackle Direct – http://bit.ly/1WrN2sG

American Bass Outlet - http://bit.ly/1XUZFea

Orvis - http://bit.ly/1XvwHS0

Columbia Performance Fishing Gear - http://bit.ly/1TRlrAo

Backcountry.com - http://bit.ly/2biXTa9

Sierra Trading Post Fishing Guide - http://bit.ly/2cbwkQp

Iboats - http://bit.ly/2bjevJh

Bulk Soft Plastics - http://ebay.to/20BRcyo

West Marine - ($15 off orders of $200 or more use promotional code: WMAFF) - http://bit.ly/1SMHV0y

Books:

Roland, M. 1998: Roland Martin's 101 Bass-Catching Secrets (Hardcover) Winchester Press; 2nd edition. ISBN: 0832904570 http://amzn.to/1HgqPZW

Striped Ostrich Fishing Books and Videos - http://bit.ly/1qI421Q

FISHING GLOSSARY

Action - Measure of rod performance that describes the elapsed time between flexion and return to straight configuration; ranges from slow to fast, with slow being the most amount of flexion; also referred to as the strength of the rod (light, medium and heavy) with light being a limber rod and heavy a stout rod; also refers to gear of reels.

Active Fish - Bass that are feeding heavily and striking aggressively.

Adaptation - Biological adjustment that increases fitness.

Algae - Simple plant organisms.

Alkalinity - Measure of the amount of acid neutralizing bases.

Alley - An opening between patches of emergent weeds; also the parallel space separating emergent weeds and the shoreline.

Amp - Measure of electrical current.

Amp Hour - Storage capacity measurement of a deep-cycle batter obtained by multiplying the current flow in amps by the hours that it is produced.

Anchor Trolley - A rigging system incorporating ropes, pulleys, and carabiners along the sides of kayaks allowing the angler to properly position his boat especially in wind or current.

Angler - Person using pole or rod and reel to catch fish.

Anti-reverse - System that prevents reels from spinning in reverse.

Backlash - Tangle of line on a bait-casting reel due to spool overrun.

Backwater - Shallow area off a river.

Bag Limit - Restriction on the number of fish that an angler may harvest in a day.

Bail - Metal, semicircular arm on an open-face spinning reel that engages the line after a cast.

Bait - An artificial lure is usually what is meant even though bait can also mean live bait.

Bait casting - Fishing with a revolving-spool reel and bait casting rod; reel mounted on topside of rod.

Baitfish - Small fish often eaten by predators.

Bar - Long ridge in a body of water.

Basic Needs - Refers to the three survival requirements of bass: reproduction, security, and food.

Bay - Major indentation in the shoreline of a lake or reservoir.

Bite - When a fish takes or touches (or hammers) a bait so that the fisherman feels it. Also known as a hit, bump, or a strike.

Black Bass - Common term used to describe several types of bass, including the largemouth, smallmouth, and spotted bass.

Blank - Fishing rod without grip, guides or finish.

Brackish - Water of intermediate salinity between seawater and freshwater.

Break - Distinct variation in otherwise constant stretches of cover, structure, or bottom type. Basically anything, that "breaks up" the underwater terrain.

Break line - A line of abrupt change in depth, bottom type, or water clarity in the feature of otherwise uniform structure. A place where there is a sudden or drastic change in the depth of the water, or weed type. This may be the edge of a creek, a submerged cliff, or even a stand of submerged weeds.

Brush line - The inside or the outside edge of a stretch of brush.

Brush pile - Usually refers to a mass of small- to medium-sized tree limbs lying in the water. Brush piles may be only one or two feet across, or they may be extremely large and they may be visible or submerged. They can be created by Mother Nature or manmade. They usually hold fish. And fishermen.

Bumping - Refers to the act of making a lure hit an object such as a log, tree, or pier piling in a controlled manner. This is often done unintentionally, but can get the same reaction from the fish. Also, a lure making contact with the bottom.

Buzz bait - Top water bait with large, propeller-type blades that churn the water during retrieve. Comprised of a lead head, rigid hook, and wire that supports one or more blades.

Cabbage - Any of several species of weeds, located above the surface or underwater, of the genus Potamogeton.

Carolina Rig - A style of terminal tackle normally used to keep a lure a foot or two (or more) off the bottom. This is most commonly used with a plastic worm, but is also used with floating crankbaits and other lures as well. A barrel slip sinker of 1/2- to 1-ounce is first slipped on the line and then a swivel is tied to the end of the line. A piece of line 18 to 30 inches long is then tied to the other end of the swivel and a hook or lure is tied to the end of this piece line. Rigged Texas style (weedless with the hook buried in the body of the bait), the combination is excellent for fishing ledges, points, sandbars, and humps. Diagram

Channel - The bed of a stream or river.

Chugger – Top water plug with a dished-out (concave or "cupped") head designed to make a splash when pulled sharply.

Clarity - Refers to the depth you are able to see an object (such as your lure) under the water.

Cold Front - A weather condition accompanied by high, clear skies, and a sudden drop in temperature.

Contact Point - The deepest position on structure where a bass angler can first effectively present his lure to bass as they migrate from deep water.

Controlled Drift - The act of using an electric motor, drift sock, or oars to allow a drift to be accomplished at a certain speed and/or direction. This term is often called "drift fishing" by most anglers.

Coontail - Submerged aquatic plant of the hornwort family typically found in hard water; characterized by stiff, forked leaves.

Cosmic Clock - The sun's seasonal effect on water and weather conditions relating to barometric pressure, wind, and cloud cover.

Count It Down - Timing a sinking lure to determine when it will reach a specified depth. This is accomplished by finding the rate of sinking of a lure in feet-per-second. Often used when fishing for suspended fish.

Cove - An indentation along a shoreline.

Cover - Natural or manmade objects on the bottom of lakes, rivers, or impoundments, especially those that influence fish behavior. Anything a fish can use to conceal itself. Examples include stick-ups, tree lines, stumps, rocks, logs, pilings, docks, weeds, boathouses, duck blinds, bushes, etc. (not to be confused with structure).

Crankbait - Typically, a lipped lure that dives under the surface during the retrieve. So-called lipless crankbaits are thin, minnow-like lures that sink at a rate of about 1-foot per second.

Dabbling - Working a lure up and down in the same spot a dozen or more times in a bush or beside a tree.

Depth finder - A sonar device, either a flasher unit or LCR recorder, used to read the bottom structure, determine depth, and in some cases actually spot the fish; also called a fish finder.

Disgorger - Device for removing hooks deeply embedded in the throat of fish.

Drag - Device on fishing reels that allows line to pay out under pressure, even though the reel is engaged; set correctly, it ensures against line breakage.

Drop-Off - A sudden increase in depth, created by gulley washes, small creek channels, land points, and the general lay of the land.

Drop Shot - A hook tied directly to the line from four-inches to four-feet above the sinker. The hook is attached from the back side or opposite the point, with a simple Palomar knot with a tag end about four or five feet long. The weight hangs and the hook is at a 90-degree angle to the line with the hook point up. The hook can be 18 to 24 inches above a bell sinker tied on with a slip-knot.

Ecology - The branch of biology dealing with the relationship between organisms and their environment.

Edge - Refers to the borders created by a change in the structure or vegetation in a lake. Some examples of edges are tree lines, weed lines, and the edge of a drop-off.

Euthrophic - Highly fertile waters characterized by warm, shallow basins.

Fan Cast - Making a series of casts only a few degrees apart to cover a half circle (more or less).

Farm Pond - Small manmade body of water.

Feeder Creek - Tributary to a stream.

Feeding Times - Certain times of the day when fish are most active. These are associated with the position of the sun and moon and are referred to as solunar tables (also called moon charts) and are predictable for any time and place. See Moon Times.

Filamentous Algae - Type of algae characterized by long chains of attached cells that give it a stringy feel and appearance.

Feeding Cycle - Certain regular intervals during which bass satisfy their appetites. Examples: Major or minor solunar periods; sunrise, sunset.

Finesse Fishing - An angling technique characterized by the use of light tackle - line, rods, reel and artificial baits (often tube worms, grubs, or other small-sized soft-plastic lures); often productive in clear, fairly uncluttered water.

Flat - An area in a body of water with little if any change in depth. Small and large, flats are generally surrounded on at least one side by deeper water, the bottom comes up to form a flat area where fish will often move up for feeding.

Flipping - (generally shortened to flippin') The technique of placing a lure in a given spot precisely, and quietly, with as little disturbance of the water as possible using an underhand cast while controlling the line with your hand.

Flipping Stick - Heavy action fishing rod, 7 to 8 feet long, designed for bass fishing.

Florida Rig - Very similar to the Texas Rig, the only difference is the weight is secured by "screwing" it into the bait.

Fly 'N Rind - Same thing as jig-and-pig - a combination of a lead head jig and pork rind trailer.

Forage - Small baitfish, crayfish and other creatures that bass eat. May also be used in the sense of the bass looking for food (foraging).

Freeboard – The distance from the waterline to the gunwales of a boat.

Front - Weather system that causes changes in temperature, cloud cover, precipitation, wind and barometric pressure.

Gear Ratio - Measure of a reels' retrieve speed; the number of times the spool revolves for each complete turn of the handle.

Grayline - Grayline lets you distinguish between strong and weak echoes. It "paints" gray on targets that are stronger than a preset value. This allows you to tell the difference between a hard and soft bottom. For example, a soft, muddy or weedy bottom returns a weaker symbol which is shown with a narrow or no gray line. A hard bottom returns a strong signal which causes a wide gray line.

Grub - A short plastic worm used with a weighted jig hook.

Gunwales - The upper side edge or side railings of a kayak or canoe. Pronounced ("Gunnels")

Habitat - The place in nature where a plant or animal species lives. The water, vegetation, and all that makes up the lake, which is where bass live. Habitat, for other creatures, is also in the woods and cities, it's basically a term used to indicate a "living area" or home environment.

Hard Bottom - Area in a body of water with a solid base - clay, gravel, rock, sand. The type of bottom that you would not sink far, if at all, were you to walk on it.

Hawg - Usually refers to a lunker-size or heavyweight bass weighing four pounds or more.

Holding Area - Structure that habitually holds three to five catchable bass.

Holding Station - Place on lake where inactive fish spend most of their time.

Honey Hole - A super fishing spot containing a number of big fish; also any place with a large concentration of keeper fish.

Horizontal Movement - The distance a fish moves while remaining at the same depth.

Hull – The main body underside of the boat. Often a different shape for different functions.

Hump - An area higher than the surrounding area. A submerged dam or island might be considered a hump.

Ichthyology - The branch of zoology that deals with fishes - their classification, structure, habits, and live history.

Inactive Fish - Bass that are in a non-feeding mood. Examples of typically inactive times: following a cold front; during a major weather change that causes a sudden rise or fall in water temperature, or when a rising lake lever is abruptly lowered.

Inside Bend - The inside line of a grass bed or a creek channel.

Isolated Structure - A possible holding spot for bass; examples include a single bush on a point; a mid-lake hump, or a large tree that has fallen into the water.

Jig - A lead head poured around a hook and featuring a skirt of rubber, plastic, or hair.

Jig-N-Pig - Combination of a lead head jig and pork rind trailer; among the most effective baits for attracting trophy-size bass.

Kayak – A vessel powered by paddling rather than a motor. Kayaks can be outfitted with many various forms of modifications for fishing.

Keeper - A bass that conforms to a specific minimum length limit established by tournament organizations and/or state fisheries department.

Lake Modification Sources - Elements that change bodies of water, such as ice action, wave action, and erosion.

Lake Zones - Designation that includes four categories: shallow water, open water, deep water, and basin.

Laydown (or Falldown) - A tree that has fallen into the water.

Light Intensity - The amount of light that can be measured at certain depths of water; the greater the intensity, the farther down the light will project. This measurement can be significantly affected by wind conditions and water clarity. In waters where light intensity is low, brightly colored lures are smart choices.

Line Guides - Rod rings through which fishing line is passed.

Lipless Crankbaits - Artificial baits designed to resemble a swimming baitfish. Such plugs vibrate and/or wobble during retrieve; some have built-in rattles. Also called swimming baits.

Live well - An aerated tank in boats used to hold fish in water until weigh-in time so that they have a better chance of survival when released. Similar to an aquarium.

Logjam - A group of horizontal logs pushed together by wind or water flow to form an obstruction. In lakes, logjams are usually found close to shore and in the backs of coves.

Loose-Action Plug - A lure with wide and slow movements from side to side.

Lunker - Normally, a bass weighing 4 pounds or more.

Micropterus Salmoides - Scientific term for largemouth bass.

Migration Route - The path followed by bass when moving from one area to another.

Milfoil - Surface-growing aquatic plants.

Mono - Short for monofilament fishing line.

Moon Times - Four phases of the moon are usually what the fisherman is concerned with. Generally the "best times" in a month occur three days prior and three days after, and include the day of the new or full moon. First quarter and second quarter periods are considered as only "good times."

Off Color - Refers to the color and or clarity of the water. Brown is muddy like from rain runoff, greenish from algae and black from tannic acid are the normal off-color conditions.

Our Hole - Proprietary term used by anglers to describe the area they intend to fish. (My hole, their hole, etc.) Though actually all holes are all angler's holes since the lakes being fished are mostly public water. It's only your hole if you get there first or own it. Otherwise it's their hole.

Outside Bend - The outside line of a creek channel or grass bed can be considered on outside bend.

Oxbow - A U-shaped bend in a river. These can also be eventually isolated into lakes.

Paddle – A propulsion tool used to move a kayak, usually a two bladed design on either end of a shaft.

Pattern - A defined set of location and presentation factors that consistently produce fish. Example: If you catch more than one fish off a pier or stick-up, then your chances of catching more bass in such places are excellent. This is commonly called "establishing a pattern".

Pegging - Putting a toothpick in the hole of a slip sinker to prevent the sinker from sliding along the line. Other items such as rubber bands slipped through the sinker have also become popular and don't snag line.

PFD - Initials that stand for Personal Floatation Device; also called a life vest/jacket.

pH - This is a measurement for liquids to determine whether they are acidic or alkaline. On a scale of one to ten, seven is considered neutral. Below seven the liquid is acidic and above seven it is alkaline. This is a factor that plays a role in the health of the lake and the fish as well as where the fish may be found in a lake.

pH Meter - Just as a thermometer measures heat and cold, a pH meter can be used to measure the acidity and alkalinity of water. The pH scale ranges from 0 to 14. Bass generally prefer water that is slightly alkaline in the 7.5 to 7.9 range. Water with a pH less than 7 is acidic. Once popular among serious bass fishermen, the device is no longer widely used.

Pick-Up - The act of a bass taking a slowly fished lure, such as a plastic worm, crawfish or lizard.

Pit - Area excavated for mining operations that fills with water.

Pitching - Presentation technique in which worms or jigs are dropped into cover at close range with an underhand pendulum motion, using a 6 ? to 71/2 foot bait casting rod. The act of pitching a bait into a pocket or under tree limbs. Similar to flipping, but requires less stealth and usually done from further distances (known as pitchin').

Pocket - A small indentation of the shoreline.

Point - A finger of land jutting into the water; deeper water is usually found just beyond the exposed tip and along the length of both sides. Fishing on and around points is often exceptionally rewarding. They almost always hold fish.

Post Front - The period following a cold front; atmosphere clears and becomes bright.

Presentation - A collective term referring to choice of type of lure, color, and size; structure targeted; amount of disturbance a bait makes when entering the water; and retrieval technique, speed, and depth used to catch fish. This refers to the circumstances and manner (speed and direction, etc.) in which a lure is presented to a fish.

Pro – Anyone who makes an income, especially a living or significant portion of their living from the sport fishing industry.

Professional Overrun - A polite term for backlash.

RAM - An accessory company featuring a ball locking system for attachment of rod holders, fish finders, GPS, etc.

Revolving-Spool Reel - Another term for bait casting reel. The spool turns during casting, unlike the spool of a spinning or spin casting reel.

Reservoir - Artificially created place where water is collected and stored; also called an impoundment.

Riprap - A man-made stretch of rocks or material of a hard composition that usually extend above and below the shoreline; often found near dams of big impoundments.

Saddle - Site where structure narrows before widening again.

Sanctuary - Deep-water bass habitat.

Scatter Point - Position along structure where bass start to separate or scatter; often found in shallow water, at or very close to a break line.

Scotty - An accessory company featuring rod holders, fish finder mounts, etc.

Short Strike - When a fish hits at a lure and misses it.

Slack Line - The loose line from the tip of the rod to the lure. This can be a slight bow in the line to an excess of line lying on the water.

Slicks - Bass not long enough to meet tournament standards; typically less than 14 inches. Such fish also are called "nubbins ", "through backs", "pop corns", "babies" and "dinks".

Slip Sinker - A lead weight with a hole through the center. Threaded on line, a slip sinker slides freely up and down.

Slough - A long, narrow stretch of water such as a small stream or feeder tributary off a lake or river.

Slow Roll – Spinner bait presentation in which the lure is retrieved slowly through and over cover objects.

Spin caster - A manner of fishing employing a push-button, closed-face spinning reel and bait casting rod; reel is mounted on the topside of the rod.

Spinner bait - A lead head lure similar in shape to an open safety-pin with a hook; other features include a rubber, plastics, or hair skirt, and one or two blades of various shapes and sizes.

Spinning - A manner of fishing employing an open-face or closed-face spinning reel an spinning rod; reel is mounted on the underside of the rod; rod guides are on the underside of the rod.

Split Shotting - Use a small #5 split-shot and crimp it about 18 inches above a light wire 1/0 or lighter small hook. Spinning tackle is a must. Small worms, three inch salt craws and others are perfect for the gentle application required. Also works well to get a small live bait down to depth.

Spook - The act of alarming a fish in a negative way. Examples: excessive noise, casting a human shadow.

Stick-Up - Stationary structure - stump, limb, section of pipe, fence post - that extends about 5 feet or less above the surface; a favorite casting target of bass fishermen.

Stragglers - Bass that remain near shore following a general migration.

Stringer - Antiquated term for a limit of fish, used by tournament anglers to indicate their catch (10-pound stringer = 10 pounds of fish. Not actually used any longer to retain bass, just a term people can't seem to stop using. (see live well).

Structure - Changes in the shape of the bottom of lakes, rivers, or impoundments, especially those that influence fish behavior. This is probably the most misunderstood word in bass fishing. Structure is a feature on the bottom of the lake. Some examples of structure are creeks, humps, depressions, sandbars, roadbeds, ledges, and drop-offs. Some examples that are not structure: a stump, tree, or brush pile (these are cover).

Suspended Fish - Bass at midlevel depths, neither near the surface nor on the bottom.

Swimming Lures - Sinking-type artificial baits designed to resemble a swimming baitfish. Such plugs vibrate and/or wobble during retrieve; some have built-in rattles. Also called lipless crankbaits.

Tail-Spinners - Compact, lead-bodied lures with one or two spinner blades attached to the tail, and a treble hook suspended from the body; designed to resemble a wounded shad; effective on schooling bass.

Taper - An area in a body of water that slopes toward deeper depths.

Terminal Tackle - Angling equipment, excluding artificial baits, attached to the end of a fishing line; examples include hooks, snaps, swivels, snap-swivels, sinkers, floats, and plastic beads.

Texas Rig - The method of securing a hook to a soft-plastic bait - worm, lizard, crawfish, so that the hook is weedless. A slip sinker is threaded onto the line and then a hook is tied to the end of the line. The hook is then inserted into the head of a worm for about one-quarter of an inch and brought through until only the eye is still embedded in the worm. The hook is then rotated and the point is embedded slightly into the worm without coming out the opposite side.

Thermocline - The layer of water where the temperature changes at least one-half a degree per foot of depth. Basically, a layer of water where rising warm and sinking cold water meet.

Tight-Action Plug - A lure with short, rapid side-to-side movement.

Tip top - Line guide at top of fishing rod.

Top Waters - Floating hard baits that create some degree of surface disturbance during retrieve.

Trailer Hook - The extra hook, or cheater hook added to a single-hook lure, such as a spinner bait or weedless spoon.

Transition - The imaginary line where one type of bottom material changes to another.

Transducer – The sonar emitting device placed in the water or inside the hull which transmits to an on screen display of a fish finder.

Treble Hook - Hook with single or bundled shaft and three points.

Triggering - Employment of any lure-retrieval technique or other fishing strategy that causes a bass to strike.

Trolling Motor - A small electric fishing motor that is used as secondary boat propulsion, for boat positioning, and to maneuver quietly in fishing areas.

Turnover - The period when the cold water on the surface of a body of water descends and is replaced by warmer water from below.

Vertical Movement - Up and down movement of fish. Can also be movement of a lure such as a spoon (vertical jigging).

Weedless - A description of a lure designed to be fished in heavy cover with a minimum amount of snagging.

Weed Line - Abrupt edge of a weed bed caused by a change in depth, bottom type, or other factor.

Worming - The act of fishing with a plastic worm, lizard, crawfish, or similar bait.

ABOUT THE AUTHOR

Chris Lutz is a former kayak fishing guide on the Potomac River and surrounding lakes.

He is the owner of Lutz Lures (www.SPARTAfishing.com), a fishing lure and kayak fishing company and blog. Chris has been fishing his whole life and specifically kayak fishing since being introduced to the paddle sports in college in 2000. He wants others to have this amazing experience too and plans to be a life-long ambassador for the sport. His mission is to help you have more fun, be a more successful kayak fisherman, and spend more quality time with your loved ones.

Larry Lutz with his two sons, Chris Lutz (the author, right), and Mike Lutz kayak fishing the Potomac River in Virginia.

Made in the USA
Middletown, DE
10 February 2023

24537933R00073